Competing with the Sylph

Competing with the Sylph

The Quest for the Perfect Dance Body

Second Edition

L. M. Vincent, M.D.

A Dance Horizons Book
Princeton Book Company, Publishers
Princeton, NJ

A Dance Horizons Book
Princeton Book Company, Publishers
POB 57
Pennington, NJ 08534

Cover Design by Eric Fowler
Interior Design by Roxanne Barrett

Printed in the United States of America

Library of Congress Cataloging-in-Publication Data

Vincent, Lawrence M.
  Competing with the sylph : the quest for the perfect dance body /
L. M. Vincent. — 2nd ed.
  p. cm.
  "A Dance horizons book."
  Includes bibliographical references and index.
  ISBN 0-916622-83-5 : $24.95. — ISBN 0-916622-82-7 (pbk.) :
$14.95
  1. Ballet dancing—Physiological aspects. 2. Women dancers—
Diseases. 3. Reducing—Physiological aspects. 4. Ballet dancing—
Psychological aspects. 5. Women—Physiology. I. Title.
RC1220.B27V56   1989
613'.0424—dc20   88-84124
                                                                              CIP

For the principal dancers in my life:
Sharon, Jordan, and Caitlin

Table of Contents

Acknowledgements
(First Edition)

Now, anxious to allow my typewriter the privacy of its own case, I am able to offer only the humblest of thanks to those largely responsible for what I place my own name upon.

First, to the many professional dancers, students, instructors, and administrators, for their cooperation and candor, as well as the following group of professionals, consultants who provided their experience, expertise, feedback, and suggestions: Richard M. Bachrach, D.O. (Osteopathy), David V. Forrest, M.D. (Psychiatry), Rose E. Frisch, Ph.D. (Epidemiology), David M. Garner, Ph.D. (Psychology), William G. Hamilton, M.D. (Orthopedics), Jack Katz, M.D. (Psychiatry), Barnard Kleiger, M.D. (Orthopedics), Edith J. Langner, M.D. (Endocrinology), Ernest Leibov, M.D. (Psychiatry), William A. Liebler, M.D. (Orthopedics), Eugene L. Lowenkopf, M.D. (Psychiatry), Alan H. Pressman (Chiropractic), Mona Shangold, M.D. (Gynecology), Robert A. Vigersky, M.D. (Endocrinology), Michelle P. Warren, M.D. (Gynecology), and Barnett Zumoff, M.D. (Endocrinology).

Clive Barnes, Alexandra Danilova, Iris Fanger, Anna Kisselgoff, John Gruen, and Marcia Siegel were generous in sharing their time and special perspectives on dance.

Robert P. Hudson, M.D., and Bernice Jackson hospitably coordinated my excursions through the Logan Clendening History of Medicine Library at the University of Kansas Medical Center.

Arthur R. Clemett, M.D., arranged the necessary time flexibility for the project, and Jim Andrews, my publisher, once again let himself be convinced.

Bill Batson and Jim Goss provided photographic services, and were fortunate enough to have Flora Ann Hall for their subject.

And finally, I am obliged to David F. White, Mark Shwayder, and Sharon Tyers, who provided the advice and support that comes only with friendship.

Acknowledgements
(Second Edition)

I am indebted to many individuals whose help and kindness made this new edition possible—some are new friends, others are second-timers.

Once again, Rose E. Frisch, Ph.D., David M. Garner, Ph.D., Jean Brooks-Gunn, Ph.D., William G. Hamilton, M.D., William A. Liebler, M.D., and Michelle P. Warren, M.D., were only a phone call away, in some cases providing me previews of articles still in manuscript form. Linda H. Hamilton, Ph.D., Barbara Drinkwater, Ph.D., and Charlotte F. Sanborn, Ph.D., were invaluable resources. Of my numerous additional medical and dance "curbside consultants," I must give particular mention to Charles Chesnut III, M.D., Sherri Hinkle, Mrs. Marian Ladre (Illaria Obidenna), Susan M. Ott, M.D., Edward Prince, M.D., Kitty C. Reeves, Tatiana Riabouchinska, Elizabeth A. Taylor, and Carol C. Teitz, M.D.

Special thanks to David M. Garner, Ph.D., and Edward Prince, M.D., for their review and insightful critiques of portions of the manuscript.

For help in tracking down case materials, prints, and articles, my thanks go to Sharon Babcock, Cindy Grant, Larry Lough, M.D., Phreddie De Lois Popp, Justin Smith, M.D., and Madeleine M. Nichols. Michael Gertley and Trudi Peek advised and arranged for photographic services, while Deborah Falik and William J. Reilly sought out specific dance photos from their files and kindly allowed me to reproduce them.

For their secretarial expertise, Myrna Anderson and Carolyn McCray deserve special kudos.

Richard Carlin of Princeton Book Company gets much of the credit for starting the ball rolling and smoothing my course. I'm also grateful to Yoram Ben-Menachem, M.D., for his enthusiastic support of my endeavors and Wendy A. Cohen, M.D., for allowing me to invade her office to usurp her computer.

And finally, the biggest "thank you" is extended to my wife, Sharon Tyers, and daughters Jordan and Caitlin, for their patience (my being late for dinner), understanding (my not getting home for dinner), indulgence (my not feeling like dinner), and interest in astronomy (my staring into space at dinner).

Introduction to the First Edition

Life is short, and the art long; the occasion fleeting; experience fallacious, and judgement difficult.

Hippocrates, *First Aphorism*

As a lover of the dance, I am vulnerable to its mystique. Truthfully, I'm all for the mystique, and would hope to be blinded by it completely for the two hours or so that I'm seated upon a red cushion in the first ring of the New York State Theatre. But I would also hope to control that mystique somewhat, just as a rheostat connected to an electric light may modulate the gradations from a full intensity of wattage to a barely discernable amber. For most of us, the artistic sensibility must be brightened and dimmed according to things of this world, mundane things such as muscles and tendons, hormones and blood sugar levels, anxieties and dreams.

Certainly the mystique will wax and wane for the dancer, whether he or she be motivated by necessity, love, an inner need or compulsion, or a spark of magic. What is evoked upon a stage may be elusive, but the sweat, dedication, denial, and pain are very real. There is nothing the least mystical about not having enough weeks of performing to be eligible for unemployment. There is nothing mystical about an injury that threatens a career for which a twenty-three year old has strived for as long as she can remember. There is nothing the least mystical about continually having to confront one's failures. The life of a dancer may or may not be rewarding, but most assuredly it will not be easy.

Throughout my exposure and association with the dance world, I accepted various aspects of the subculture as "part and parcel" of dancing. My medical bent was directed primarily toward physical injuries encountered by dancers, generally problems of an orthopedic nature. There was a security in such a narrow focus: troublesome considerations outside of the specific domain could be justifiably cast aside, taken for granted as part of a framework within which one must of necessity operate. But then the lighting changed. Vividly I recall the specific moment when I became conscious of a different angle of vision.

While walking down Sixth Avenue in New York, I passed a young ballet scholarship student from a company ballet school. I had seen her and others like her many times before, on my daily jaunts to and from the hospital. Hair pulled severely and pinned into a chignon, she walked turned out, wore a bulky sweater, jeans, and clogs, and carried an overstuffed dance bag by a strap across her shoulder. On that particular day I did not see a starry-eyed ballet student coming from her adagio class; I saw a pale, gaunt seventeen-year-old with dark circles under her eyes and a downcast gaze. Her unhealthy visage bore none of the physical exuberance and vitality usually associated with exercise. She looked terrible.

As it happened, she had danced seven hours that day and had eaten only an orange and a slice of mango. Later I also learned that she had been inducing vomiting on a regular basis for three months in an effort to attain her "ideal" dancing weight. Concern with weight and diet, with looking like a ballerina—one of those idiosyncrasies that are "part and parcel" of the dance world—had become a vicious, self-destructive obsession.

To assume that artistic considerations are in any way linked to health considerations is totally unrealistic and naive. A choreographer may be at liberty to manifest concern for a dancer only insofar as that person conforms to his or her artistic vision: maintenance and preservation of health need not be the top priority. Individuals are not only forgotten with the passage of time; in some circumstances they are expendable commodities in the present.

This is not to suggest that artists should have medical sensibilities and vice versa, a swap that might just result in riveting dialogue among physicians, but pretty lousy art for everybody else. The point is that much of the responsibility for good health always rests with the individual. But paradoxically, in our health-conscious society, ill-advised health practices continue to abound, the result of exploitation, ignorance, and a sacrifice of common sense to a variety of dictates that may in themselves be distorted and arbitrary.

Whether one is a fashion model, a homemaker, an athlete, or a blue-collar worker, one is likely to be victimized to some extent by a culture obsessed with thinness, youth, and beauty. While dancers are not alone in the not-infrequent bartering of their physical well-being, by focusing our gaze upon them we can see quite clearly how difficulties ranging from poor weight control to menstrual dysfunction may be both self-inflicted and self-perpetuated.

One cannot consider health in its broadest sense without an awareness of its setting; the values and assumptions implicit in a particular social context provide a useful perspective on *why* rather than *how* difficulties may arise. Thus, I concern myself here with more than matters strictly medical and depart substantially from the constraints of standard scientific writing in the hope of conveying a "feel" for the subculture that serves as a model. I have attempted, then, to integrate current medical knowledge from a variety of disciplines as it relates specifically to the health of dancers, in a manner both palatable and comprehensible.

Casting the mystique completely by the wayside, I will admit that—given the choice—I appreciate the beauty of a well-functioning, healthy body more than the beauty of a ballet line. In the sense that this is a subjective judgement, my perspective is slightly biased. However, did I feel in the slightest degree that the two were mutually exclusive, I never would have embarked upon the writing of this book.

L. M. Vincent, M.D.
Kansas City/New York City

Introduction to the Second Edition

Truth is never pure and rarely simple.

Oscar Wilde

It has been nearly ten years since I passed that young ballet scholarship student walking down Sixth Avenue. At the time, medical and scientific journals offered little information about the menstrual disorders of elite female athletes or sociocultural influences on eating problems. In fact, eating disorders seemed almost esoteric.

Virtually everyone today recognizes that dancers and certain other athletes share a significant incidence of menstrual and eating difficulties. More important, people appreciate that these women are not aberrations; they are simply highly visible examples, reminders in the flesh of what our society deems beautiful and where that aesthetic may lead us. Terms such as "anorexia nervosa" and "bulimia" have been reduced to the commonplace, demystified while remaining misunderstood.

The causes and implications of menstrual dysfunction and eating disorders in athletic and weight-preoccupied women are being investigated with a passion. There is now an impressive body of literature concerning these and related topics; in truth, enough material to make this author's head spin. In the meantime, while the researchers have been doggedly at work, the next generation of dancers has emerged. They have inherited the studios, the *barre* work, and the center combinations unaltered from their predecessors. And of course, the mirror is also part of their legacy.

The dancers, ever-focused on the mirror and what it reveals about their body in space, seem undistracted by the commotion, the new spotlight coming not from the wings but from the dissecting microscope. No meager number of them have participated in more than class and productions: they have filled out forms, responded to questionnaires, and been interviewed (so have their mothers). They have charted their temperature, their periods, their calories. They have had their heart rate monitored, their urine collected, and their blood drawn. They have been weighed on dry land and underwater, measured with calipers, and exercised on treadmills to the point of exhaustion.

The ongoing research has far-reaching implications in a variety of scientific and medical disciplines. To be gained is a more thorough understanding of basic physiological mechanisms and how our environment influences them. More important, the research will clarify the risks and benefits of intensive exercise and leanness in women, ways of avoiding the downside consequences, and appropriate therapies if troubles should arise. The goal is not just a healthier dancer, but a healthier person.

For now, there are areas of controversy; the issues are complex and multifactorial. Fortunately for most of us, however, those speculations and debates about occurrences at the cellular level are not relevant. Active women are well enough aware of what is happening to their bodies—what they need to know is *why* it is happening, not precisely *how* it is happening.

For the general reader, well-integrated material from disparate scientific disciplines has always been hard to come by. Specialty journals are not readily accessible to nonspecialists, who are usually bewildered by their contents anyway. Alternatively, the media have not always done a commendable job in this arena. Examples abound of well-intentioned but shoddy journalism, dissemination of misinformation, and even blatant exploitation. In fairness, journalists who tackle these issues end up with a fuller notepad than they bargained for. They are confronted with highly technical information, much of it conflicting and sometimes controversial, and they often lack the expertise to place it in the proper perspective. To make matters worse, constraints upon print space and air time frequently dictate a brevity that makes accurate reporting difficult, if not impossible.

From its inception, I viewed *Competing with the Sylph* as an informational bridge between the scientific and nonscientific communities. I allowed myself time and space to explain basic concepts and establish the framework for what was to follow. I also indulged my personal inclination toward a format and style flexible enough to accommodate digressions and other tidbits for readability. I did not intend to produce an exhaustive review, but one that maintained a reasonable level of information and conveyed a sense of perspective. Nor did I wish to confine myself to an audience of dancers—the book was intended for all weight-preoccupied individuals, which includes nearly everyone. That the first edition was well received by a diverse audience has provided me more than enough personal gratification for sustenance through the sometimes tedious process of revision.

Accordingly, I have revised and updated most of the previous sections as well as included new material. For the most part, the words of the dancers themselves are unchanged, as I believe they still reflect their world today as they did a decade ago.

Competing with the Sylph is meant primarily to inform, but along the way it is likely to disturb or reassure, as the case may be. Readers, from the merely curious to those who are themselves involved, will identify with the information contained herein to varying degrees. It is my hope that all can benefit from insight into complex issues that affect us or those we care about. If the simple dieter or the aspiring ballerina must ever make personal choices, let them be informed ones.

L. M. Vincent, M.D.
Issaquah, Washington

1 Before the Mirror

The Subculture: Generalizations and Biases

For quite some time, a six-pack of Tab sat untouched on the bottom shelf of my refrigerator, reminding me of the perils of stereotyping.

Now I don't particularly care for Tab, but after months of interviewing dancers, I had become somewhat habituated to the subtleties of the subculture. I had become accustomed to feeling gluttonous, stretching my masseter muscles around an overstuffed pastrami sandwich while a dancer sat demurely nearby, daintily spooning up yogurt or nibbling on some fruit or greens. In fact, I have to strain my memory to conjure the image of a ballet dancer drinking regular cola or using granulated sugar in tea or coffee (some would use honey). What echoes in my mind is the simple request that invariably followed a coffee order: "Do you have Sweet 'N Low?"

Which explains why I bought the Tab. In preparation for an interview, I made a special effort to be hospitable and accommodating. Admittedly it was a bit presumptuous, not unlike stocking up on caviar and vodka for a Russian houseguest.

"Would you like a diet cola?" I offered.

When the dancer replied in the negative, I was noticeably taken aback. Perhaps she had heard wrong.

"It's *Tab*," I reiterated.

"No, thank you," said the dancer, "I brought my own." And from a blue canvas dance bag she pulled out a Dr. Pepper. Sugar-free.

Nondancers have often commented to me how they are able to spot dancers walking down the street. One medical colleague perceived this as a brilliant clinical diagnosis, a stroke of deduction worthy of Sherlock Holmes, but in fact all of us carry badges of our respective subcultures, showing by our clothes, mannerisms, or speech who and what we are. One would be hard pressed to find a certified public accountant who wore her hair in a chignon, walked with external rotation of the hips (Figure 1) and carried a dance bag. Certainly one could predict the occupation of my medical friend from his white coat and its attendant paraphernalia, the Cross pen and pocket flashlight in one pocket, and a stethoscope tucked into, but revealingly exposed, in another.

Dancers belong to a very special community. In the most important sense they are bound together by the common experience of dance itself: tradition, technique, discipline, purpose.[1] Whether separated by miles or even continents, dancers will do the same or similar exercises, hear much of the same music; each will know the feel of the wood floor, the pain of pushing for a bit more extension, the satisfaction of accomplishment, the frustration of failure. The experience transcends all levels of living. The hopeful may not yet know the curtain calls or applause bestowed upon the soloist, but both will sew elastic on their slippers, wash their tights in the sink, carry Bandaids and lambswool, be annoyed if they find themselves opposite the break of the mirror in class, and probably use more acrylic floor wax on their *pointe* shoes than on their floors.[2]

The crux of many of the dilemmas of the professional dancer is the precariousness of simultaneously being athlete and interpretive artist. In terms of major athletic performance demands (including neuromuscular and physical factors, mental and psychometric factors, and environmental factors), classical ballet has been ranked second out of sixty-one sports (right behind football).[3] But all dancers have ranked second in a different

1. For glimpses of the dance experience in professional ballet companies, see Forsythe, S., Kolenda, P. M. (1966), Competition, cooperation, and group cohesion in the ballet company, *Psychiatry, 29*, 123–145; Mazo, J. H. (1974) *Dance is a contact sport,* New York: Da Capo Press; Stevens, F. (1976), *Dance as life: A season with American Ballet Theatre,* New York: Harper & Row; Gordon, S. (1983), *Off balance: The real world of ballet,* New York: Pantheon.

2. Many dancers enhance the usually short lifespan of *pointe* shoes by hardening them with multiple applications of clear acrylic floor wax.

3. Nicholas, J. A. (1976), Risk factors in sports medicine and the orthopedic system: An overview, *Journal of Sports Medicine, 3,* 243–259.

Figure 1. Take away the dance bag and the chignon, and the walk is still a dead giveaway. The walking apparatus of the ballet dancer is not mutated; rather the peculiar stride results from external rotation of the hips transplanted to the street. *Disadvantages*: (1) aesthetic considerations; (2) possible calamities on stairwells if not modified when wearing high heels; (3) hindrance of maximum running velocity; (4) possible contribution to over-stretching of the posterior tibiales tendons. *Advantages*: (1) comfort (force of habit); (2) badge of peer-group identification, particularly for younger dancers; (3) ability to walk silently even while wearing corduroy pants. (Photo by William Batson)

category—in percentage of unemployment in the labor force of writers, artists, and entertainers (right behind actors).[4] Few sports competitors (one thinks of gymnasts and figure skaters as exceptions) not only undergo rigorous continual training from an early age onward, but also must conform to aesthetic demands of a visual art form. Both the football defensive tackle defending the goal line and the tenor bellowing Puccini are allowed the freedom of resembling beer barrels.

The adoption of a dance life-style may often be narrowing and restrictive, entailing sacrifices that the run-of-the-mill athlete need not make. Not only may the commitment to intensive training begin at a young age, but for the most part training is uninterrupted and often exclusive. Unlike the football or baseball player, the dancer has no off-season or spring training. From the fledgling to the famous, there is always the class, regardless of season, day in and day out. Agnes de Mille, like every other aspiring young dancer, quickly learned:

> ... the first all-important dictate of ballet dancing—never to miss the daily practice, hell or high water, sickness or health, never to miss the barre practice; to miss meals, sleep, rehearsals even but not the practice, not for one day ever under any circumstances, except on Sundays and during childbirth.[5]

Many professional athletes, as well as amateurs of Olympic caliber, acquire their training in conjunction with college, the military, or even a professional career outside of their athletic discipline. The classical ballet dancer will more likely be called upon to burn the bridge of higher formal education in the furtherance of her chosen field. Despite the growing number of university-affiliated dance programs, university graduates are by and large "too old" to be accepted by a major classical ballet company. The dominating trend is for the youngster to develop and travel through the ranks of a performing arts school or a highly competitive company school.[6] Not uncommonly, young classical dancers who come to New

---

4. National Endowment for the Arts (1976, April), *Employment and unemployment of artists: 1970–1975*, Division Report No. 1, Washington D.C.: GPO. In more recent reports, the data base for dancers has been too small for meaningful (statistically significant) comparison.

5. de Mille, A. (1952), *Dance to the piper*. Boston: Little, Brown, p. 54.

6. How competitive? Sherrie Hinkle of the School of American Ballet reports that only one in ten of aspiring students are accepted into the summer or winter sessions. According to Jennifer Dunning (1985), in *But first a school: The first fifty years of the School of American Ballet*, (New York: Viking), only 5 percent of the girls who begin training at SAB at eight will graduate nine years later.

York City from elsewhere finish high school in an accelerated, condensed program (four years into three), obtain high-school equivalence by correspondence or proficiency exams, or forgo the diploma altogether.

Not that an academic curriculum vitae is very meaningful for a dancer, but then a career in dance is not particularly noteworthy for job opportunities, financial security, or perhaps most important, longevity. A football player's career days may be numbered (or curtailed early by injury), but the practical benefits of the professional game include high salaries, opportunities for off-season and post-retirement employment, life insurance, major medical coverage and dental insurance, and a pension. Contrast this with the not unusual case of a ballet soloist in her early thirties who faces the ending of a successful career with little education, borderline financial status, no skills unrelated to dance, and perhaps no family of her own. With respect to practical matters, giving a dance career the hard sell takes quite an imagination.

Within the dance subculture, individuals are subjected to variable influences, and dancers themselves may be likely to stress the differences more than similarities. Just as all dancers are—or perceive the need to be—thinner than the average person, classical dancers must be the thinnest of all types of dancers. Likewise, dancers in the highly competitive major companies in New York are generally thinner than nonprofessionals, or than regional or European dancers. Modern and jazz dancers usually have more flexibility in their training; they may realistically begin dance studies at a later age than ballet dancers, and a successful career for them does not as often preclude higher education.

As an illustration, consider a comparison of the educational status of members of a ballet versus a modern company, both located in New York City and both international renowned. In 1978, of the ninety-member New York City Ballet, only five dancers had attended college, and all of these were male.[7] The situation was quite different in the Martha Graham Dance Company. Ten of twelve females had attended college, and nine of eleven males had some college credit. Of the remaining four company members, three were of European origin and had accomplished course work equivalent to early college.[8] In a more recent survey of thirty-two

The survivors of this intense pyramid system, the hundred or so full-time Advanced Division students (age fourteen and up), face the prospect of an average of five or six New York City Ballet Company corps or apprentice slots opening each year. Fortunately, most of these highly competent graduates will find gainful dance employment somewhere else.

7.   Information furnished by the New York City Ballet.

8.   Information furnished by the Martha Graham Dance Company.

female dancers from four national American ballet companies, only 68 percent had completed high school.[9] Another recent survey of more than two hundred female dancers revealed that, at the beginning of their careers, 62 percent of female ballet dancers had some high school or a diploma, while 57 percent of the female modern dancers began their careers with a college degree or graduate work.[10]

Obviously a comparison of a thirty-year-old modern dancer in a company of twenty with'an eighteen-year-old ballet dancer in a corps of fifty is not a fair one. One can easily discern, though, how dance stereotypes arise, particularly when they are colored by biases, rivalry, and chauvinism. One modern dancer with whom I spoke was quite harsh regarding her classical counterparts. Her basic argument was that ballet dancers "don't have other lives or well-formed personalities," possess a "herd instinct and mentality," and "wear blinders." When I gave equal time to a ballet dancer, she countered quite matter-of-factly with, "Everyone knows that modern dancers are just frustrated ballerinas." From my vantage point, the score is now tied. Whether there are more girls in ballet with blinders on than frustrated ballerinas in modern dance does not seem to me a fruitful subject for debate. What we shall see, however, is that much more than personality determines one's dance style preference, as well as success.

The Obsession

No one is free who is a slave to the body.

Seneca (c. 4 BC–AD 65)

As regards weight, I divide females into two groups. First, there are the so-called "naturally thin" women who maintain a svelte body line without worrying much about food intake. And then there is the vast

9.   Hamilton L. H., Brooks-Gunn, J., Warren, M. P., Hamilton W. G.(1988), The role of selectivity in the pathogenesis of eating disorders in ballet dancers, *Medicine and Science in Sports and Exercise, 20,* 560–565.

10.   Wallach, E. (1988), Life after performing: Career transitions for dancers, *Update: Dance/USA, 5,* (No. 5), 5–11.

majority. Aside from the common preoccupation with food, the latter group also shares a stomach-felt resentment for the former. Some of the resentment is probably undeserved, since a good number of those envied struggle as much as the rest, but are just more discreet about it. Regardless of one's classification, most will view themselves on the heavy side of the line. Consider the results of a *Glamour* magazine survey. Of more than thirty thousand respondents, 75 percent of women indicated that they were "too fat"; only 15 percent considered themselves "just right."[11]

If obsession with fat is a national pastime, then surely dancers are Olympic contenders. One might argue that dancers talk about, refer to, or pine over food more than anything else, from the succinct "I'm fat" to the more winsome "I wish I could lose a pound from the weekend," to academic diatribes on dieting methods and physiology. But whether or not the words are spoken, there is always the mirror. Watch a dancer scrutinize herself in the mirror, probing her stomach, hips, and thighs with her fingertips, appraising herself from various angles. In her eyes is the glitter of the true believer on a search-and-destroy mission; she's going after that fat with the furor and frenzy with which one pursues roaches in the kitchen. An eighteen-year-old ballet student describes the compulsion:

> When I look into the mirror I get so distracted I can't even concentrate when I don't think I look halfway decent. It's like going to work and not brushing your hair, looking sloppy. It's in the same category as wearing a clean leotard, pinning your leotard so the line looks good. It's presenting yourself.

Dancers are justifiably preoccupied with weight, and the subculture guarantees its own peer-group pressure and reinforcement. The concern—subtly pervasive and unavoidable—starts from the first step into the dance studio. With some amusement, an ex-ballet dancer related to me how her son's first ballet class affected him. The nine-year-old, with one hour's immersion in the subculture, came home for dinner and refused his favorite dessert. He, like many other perceptive and impressionable initiates, began the ritual of dieting with his first *plié*.

> I never had a weight problem at all, but I got to New York—and I've always been slim—and the school never told me to lose weight . . . and all of a sudden, everyone else around me was on a diet to

11. *Glamour* (1984, February), pp. 198–201, 251–252.

lose weight. And when I think about it now—for no apparent reason—I felt I had to, I had to go on a diet. I had to stop eating meat. I had to stop having ice cream or cookies whenever I felt like it, and I had to lose weight. When I really didn't, but just because everybody else did.

Ballet dancer, age twenty (5'7," 117 pounds)

Inseparable from the obsession is the fact that the weight standard for dancers is different from that set for most people, much leaner than that suggested in charts, and much lighter than most women set as their reasonable dieting goal. Nondancers thus often find dancers' complaints about weight a bit hard to swallow. A five-foot, five-inch ballet dancer will bemoan her natural disposition to obesity, only to disclose that the most she's ever weighed is a paltry—though horrifying to her—112 pounds. Hearing this—both sympathy and empathy vanishing like a coin from a magician's palm—a 150-pound woman might have to combat her own natural disposition to stomp on the dancer's toes.

Obviously a dancer's weight must be considered in the context of her profession. From the outset, dancers must conform to more stringent standards, operate with a different set of aesthetic rules, look through fat-colored lenses, so to speak. Although this may be a distortion from generally accepted norms, it is very much a reality in the dance world, and doctors who routinely see dancers treat it as such. A New York City physician is matter-of-fact on the subject:

> I have two girls overweight by [the choreographer's] standards. Now they're not overweight by medical standards, but they are overweight by professional standards. I put them on diets.

The dancers themselves accept the reality to such a degree that the abnormal becomes normal to them. As one company member put it:

> A lot of us here have been doing this for such a long time . . . you lose a vision of what a woman should look like. And you might see someone walking down the street who has a beautiful body for a normal person, and you would think, "Oh, she looks a little heavy."

It takes all sizes and shapes to populate the world, and we seldom question the reality of thinness in dance. There are many justifications for slenderness, some better than others, but all in some way contributing to our current notion of what dancers are supposed to look like. The bottom line is undoubtedly aesthetic, and that's pretty hard to argue with. In the words of a dance instructor and choreographer:

> I think a thinner body is more attractive to look at than one of those Rubenesque-looking numbers. But some people don't. But when it's in a pair of pink tights, and you have all those bulges coming out, then I think it should be kept at home.

George Balanchine once stated that he liked long women for his choreography because he could "see more."[12] Whatever the artistic preferences, there just isn't much of a premium for obesity on the dance stage.

Once the aesthetic criteria are established, practical and technical matters come into play. A former principal ballerina finds that:

> . . . the technical demands nowadays made of females are tremendous compared to what they were. We're working on a tremendously high level of refinement and technique, so we're looking for a body that can endure more, that looks better.

Professional demands include a pleasing line, a suitable appearance (or sometimes the ability to fit in costumes), a weight that can be lifted (this depends upon the size and strength of available males), and usually a reasonable degree of uniformity (a six-footer in a line of five-footers is pretty distracting). A former dancer gives yet another reason, not particularly either accurate or important, but nonetheless one of my favorites: "Photographs add seven pounds. On stage you always look fatter."

In any case, there are plenty of reasons why dancers have to be thin, should one bother to ask. But there are many reasons why the aesthetic considerations of dance should not be given carte blanche. The pertinent question is not why dancers have to be thin; rather, it is "how thin is thin"? As I mentioned, it is difficult to dispute an artistic judgement; yet there's substantial variation in the fine tuning of what we consider fat and thin, all of which is inextricably tied up in what we refer to as "beauty." Not that I think there will be much of a market in the forseeable future for obese ballet dancers; still, let us cast aside our biases (as well as our knowledge of the exigencies of the dance world today) and assume a broader perspective. We might benefit by recognizing the arbitrariness, and even folly, of any ideal concept of beauty. Aesthetic fine tuning, in

12. From interview in Gruen, J. (1975), *The private world of ballet*, New York: Penguin, p. 282.

fact, may be quite coarse, and the establishment of any ideal rather presumptuous.[13]

A Crash Course in Beauty

If all our women were to become as beautiful as the Venus dé Medici, we should for a time be charmed; but we should soon wish for variety; and as soon as we had obtained variety, we should wish to see certain characters a little exaggerated beyond the then existing common standard.

Charles Darwin, *The Descent of Man*

By today's standards, Venus is a tad chunky, and a well-intentioned friend might even advise her to enroll at Weight Watchers. But consider another Venus (Figure 2), this one of Willendorf, the oldest known representation of the human form. Discovered on the banks of the Danube, and dating back to the Paleolithic period, this obese woman with enormous breasts, protruding belly, and monolithic thighs, exemplifies the taste for epic chubbiness that persisted in the Neolithic period, prehistoric Greece, Babylonia, and in Egyptian sculptures.

Whether fat women predominated or were deemed desirable, or whether the obesity was an artistic convention symbolizing abundance and fertility, we can't be completely sure. But we do know that even today in certain societies, obesity is much admired, even to the extent of being considered a secondary sexual characteristic. A fat body may connote a strong body and since only women of leisure can afford the luxury of immobilization, overfed women may represent the state of being well-to-do, and hence, part of the "beautiful people." In some cultures on the African continent, brides-to-be actually go through excessive fattening. The "coming out" of these debutantes consists of "going into" special houses for fattening, where they are secluded for periods ranging from

---

13.   For further reading on ideals of beauty and their ramifications, see Banner, L. (1983), *American beauty*, New York: Knopf; Brownmiller, S. (1984), *Femininity*, New York: Fawcett; Schwartz, H. (1986), *Never satisfied*, New York: Free Press.

Figure 2. As an illustration that fashions change with the times (in this case, over a period of twenty-thousand-and-some-odd years), compare the looks of the Venus of Willendorf (the stony-faced one on the left) and Twiggy (Leslie Hornby, circa 1967). (Photos courtesy of Naturhistorisches Museum Wien and Wide World Photos)

several weeks to years (depending on their wealth), not unlike ducks destined to donate their livers for pâté de foie gras.

Attitudes toward fat in the most elemental sense depend upon the availability of food, on whether or not nature smiles or frowns as far as nutritional prosperity is concerned. From the long-range historical stand-

point, nature's disposition has been quite sullen, if not downright vindictive. We do not usually ponder, as we weigh the merits of the spinach
salad against those of the Jarlsburg, avocado, and sprouts on whole-
wheat, that for most of the people much of the time, the task has been
much simpler—just to get enough of anything. Only when food is abundant can we indulge in gluttony and satiation, or even more important,
afford the luxury of dieting and self-imposed starvation.

On this side of the body spectrum, various cultures have gone slightly
overboard in their reaction against obesity. We know that the ancient
Greeks envied their predecessors, the Cretans, who were supposed to
have known of a drug that allowed them to eat all they wanted, yet remain
thin. The Spartans as well as the Athenians were sticklers about fat
(Socrates danced every morning to keep his figure) and the Roman ladies
at the time of the Empire evidently suffered to keep as slim as reeds. In
the sixteenth century, Montaigne wrote that women could swallow sand
in order to ruin their stomachs and acquire a pale complexion.

In more modern times, a certain degree of indecisiveness has been the
hallmark, with the pendulum swinging from one extreme to the other in
periods of relatively (historically speaking) few years. At the turn of the
twentieth century, a buxom woman was in order. Consider the complaint
of the French physician Heckel, who wrote the following in 1911:

> One must mention here that aesthetic errors of a worldly nature to
> which all women submit, may make them want to stay obese for
> reasons of fashionable appearance. It is beyond a doubt that in order
> to have an impressive décolleté, each woman feels herself duty
> bound to be fat around the neck, over the clavicle and in her breasts.
> Now it happens that fat accumulates with greatest difficulty in these
> places, and one can be sure, even without examining such a woman,
> that the abdomen and the hips, and the lower members are hope-
> lessly fat. As to treatment, one cannot obtain weight reduction of
> the abdomen without the woman sacrificing in her spirits the upper
> part of her body. To her it is a true sacrifice because she gives up
> what the world considers beautiful.[14]

In the 1920s, a flat-chested, lean, and angular creature took over. After
another twenty years, the rotund look was again the symbol of attractive-

---

14. Heckel, F. (1911), *Les grandes et petites obésités*, Paris: Masson, as quoted in H. Bruch
(1973), *Eating disorders: Obesity, anorexia nervosa, and the person within*, New York: Basic
Books, pp. 18–19.

ness. So when Twiggy hit the scene in the mid-sixties (5 feet, 7 inches and 92 pounds in her prime), exemplifying for adolescents throughout the world what they might aspire to look like when they grew up, she was merely another variant of body overhauling in conformance to ever-changing ideals (Figure 2).[15]

More disturbing than the mere arbitrariness of a concept of beauty is the awesome health consequences that previous generations of women have had to endure. The attempt to convert the female contour into an hourglass with the instrument of torture known as the corset is an appropriate example. From the 1820s on, the stylish waist circumference was 18 inches (Figure 3). The tiny-waisted yet stout woman—a species that had never before existed in nature—evolved virtually overnight, thanks to the crinoline reinforced with whalebone and steel (tight straps were used earlier, but the more barbarous devices came into vogue after 1854, with the whalebone variety marking an advanced degree of female disfigurement). Women tolerated and even sought mutilation that reminds one of binding the feet, a custom which persisted for more than a thousand years in China.

Aside from clawing the flesh and displacing internal organs (the hazards of splitting steel stays were ever-present, particularly for those who exercised while corseted), the corset undoubtedly decreased the volume of food ingested through pure mechanical pressure, while serving at the same time as a strong psychological inducement to restrict intake. Even when the harm of corsets had been recognized, the idiocy was continued on moral grounds, for an unlaced woman had come to be regarded as licentious, a veritable vessel of sin. One such unlaced and barefooted symbol of heresy was Isadora Duncan, who integrated an approach to dance with a crusade for corset consumer protection. That women were eventually freed from the grip, however, was probably not so much the result of Isadora's efforts as of good fortune thoroughly disguised. Only after the War Industries Board revealed that unbinding American women

---

15.   Standards of beauty, of course, involve much more than the mere amount and distribution of body fat. I am reminded of Gelsey Kirkland, who admitted to acquiring silicone injections in her lips in her autobiography, apparently in an attempt to emulate Suzanne Farrell, then the darling of George Balanchine (See Kirkland, G. & Lawrence, G. (1986), *Dancing on my grave*, New York: Doubleday). This particular physical modification has an amusing nineteenth-century precedent. According to Banner, *American beauty*, op. cit., p. 49, fashionable women went to elaborate lengths to attain the small "bee-stung" mouth, then considered the most important feature of the beautiful face. Without silicone and plastic surgery at their disposal, they resorted to repeating in sequence a series of *p* words ("peas," "prunes," and "prisms" were the most popular), which had the effect of rounding and puckering the mouth. Photographers of this period did not ask their female subjects to say "cheese," but rather to repeat the *p* words.

Figure 3. In this parody of fashionables by Robert Cruikshank, appropriately entitled "Monstrosities of 1827," the wasp-waisted women gallivanting in Hyde Park are escorted by less impressively squeezed, but nonetheless corset-constricted, dandies. (From the author's collection)

would release twenty-eight thousand tons of steel, enough to build two World War I battleships, did liberation from lacing get into gear.[16]

A Somewhat Different Look at "the Look"

Bright little bird bones, delicate bird sinews! She was all fire and steel wire. There was not an ounce of spare flesh on her skeleton, and the life force used and used her body until she died of the fever of moving, gasping for breath, much too young ... Her trunk was small and stripped of all anatomy but the ciphers of adolescence, her arms and legs relatively long, the neck extraordinarily long and mobile ... Without any way being sensual, being, in fact, almost sexless, she suggested all exhilaration, gaity, and delight.

Agnes de Mille, *Dance to the Piper*

16.   Rudofsky, B. (1974), *The unfashionable human body*, New York: Doubleday, Anchor Press, p. 189.

This twentieth-century description of Anna Pavlova by Agnes de Mille might well be a voice from the nineteenth century preserved intact. More striking than the continued presence of Romantic ballets in modern repertory is the influence Romanticism has on our current concept of the look of the ballerina. Certainly the era of the Romantic ballet must be seen in terms of the larger Romantic Movement in art and literature, and it was these times that resurrected and nurtured the sylph.[17] Representing lightness, ethereality, and spirituality, the sylph still connotes the "dreamy silhouette" to which many a ballet dancer may aspire. With a bit of medical-historical irreverance, we might examine the Romantic roots to illustrate why the sylph, not unlike the corseted woman, might have difficulty obtaining health insurance.

A perusal of a good part of the literature of the nineteenth century reads like copy for a cough syrup advertisement. Heroes and heroines hacked, shivered, chilled, coughed up blood, and fevered themselves into oblivion, albeit rather gracefully. Not that lung ailments, specifically tuberculosis (then called consumption), accounted for the Romantic Movement, but undoubtedly the disease contributed significantly to the gloom and weepiness that marked the tear-tracked face of the period. This mysterious affliction enlisted the greatest of sympathies and was a quite useful literary device—consumption was commonly believed to chiefly affect sensitive natures (it was once thought to enhance creativity). In addition, the tragedy of youth and beauty fading conferred a refined, physical charm upon the stricken as they succumbed to a painless, poetic death. Before leaving this earth, one first had to go into decline, until substance gradually dissolved into spirituality like houselights going into a slow fade.

Few diseases today have such positive connotations or artistic merit (one thinks of hypoglycemia, which is a bit trendy in dance circles, or perhaps various and sundry neuroses, celebrated in the humor of Woody Allen). But tuberculosis was the darling of art and literature for half a century before losing its poetic luster, and it was, conveniently, as prevalent then as tendonitis is in dance classes or among joggers these days. There were many notables who coughed, lay down, and were counted in the dismal parade of their art, among them several Brontës, Elizabeth Barrett Browning, John Keats, and Robert Louis Stevenson.

17. According to Banner, *American beauty*, op. cit., p. 46, the etherealized woman actually first emerged in the late Middle Ages, a product of Eastern influences brought back to Europe by the Crusaders and of the veneration of women that was central to the cult of chivalry.

Aside from the creators themselves, models were similarly affected. Marguerite Gauthier, of *Camille* fame, was based upon Alphonsine Plessis, one-time mistress of Alexandre Dumas *fils*, a fashionable courtesan who led a whirlwind social life and was the center of worshipping attention wherever she went until her death of consumption at twenty-three. Mimi of *La Bohème* was in real life a flower girl in Paris who came to live with Henri Munger before also succumbing to the disease (he wrote *Scènes de la Vie de Bohème*, the basis of the Puccini opera). Janet Burden and Elizabeth Siddal (married to Gabriel Rossetti), prominent models for pre-Raphaelite paintings, were both fragile, languishing, and long-limbed, and both, as befit unhealthy symbols of the era, had tuberculosis.[18]

Thus, art imitated life and life subsequently imitated the imitation to mock itself, as ethereality became the vogue. Observed Dumas:

> In 1823 and 1824 it was the fashion to suffer from the lungs; everybody was consumptive, poets especially; it was good form to spit blood after each emotion that was at all sensational, and to die before reaching the age of thirty.[19]

Paleness, not glowing health, was the fashionable attribute of women, as men cultivated a passion for delicate, languishing companions threatened with impending death. The use of rouge was abandoned in favor of the whitening powders. Regardless of season, women were draped in various light materials, such as unbleached batiste and embroidered organdy muslin. Weakness and refinement became synonomous (see Figures 4 and 5):

> The generation of 1830 liked its women to be charming, graceful, and delicate. It again became the fashion to be pale and to faint continually . . . no woman in society went without her lorgnette, which lent her an additional touch of amiable helplessness; and if she ate little at table, and put her glove by mistake into her glass, it all helped to show how ethereally she was constituted. . . . A woman who thought anything of herself could at the most allow herself to

---

18. For a fascinating account of the history of tuberculosis, from which much of the material on consumption and the Romantic age is derived, see Dubos, R. & Dubos, J. (1952), *The white plague*, Boston: Little, Brown.

19. From the memoirs of Alexandre Dumas, as quoted in Dubos & Dubos, *White plague*, op. cit., p. 59.

Figure 4. "Following the Fashion" is James Gillray's parody of the sensational "new look" of 1793 (whose introduction was credited to Lady Charlotte Campbell), which sought to imitate the clinging drapery of classical statuary. Gillray seems less offended by the ethereal, fashionable "Soul without a Body" than by the fat and unwieldy lower-class emulator. (From the author's collection)

nibble a few sweetmeats; in 1825 she began to require water to rinse her mouth, and in 1830 bowls to wash her fingers in.[20]

The desire to appear pale was most assuredly not a particularly healthy impulse. Food habits, even of the prosperous, were far from conducive to good health for a number of reasons. Because of the obstacles of season and distribution, it was not always an easy matter to get fresh milk and vegetables. Also, there were certain prejudices against some types

20. Fischel, O. & Von Boehn, M. (1909), *Modes and manners of the nineteenth century as represented in the pictures and engravings of the times,* M. Edwards, trans., New York: Dutton, Vol. 2, p. 149.

DROPSY *courting* CONSUMPTION.

Figure 5. "Dropsy Courting Consumption," Thomas Rowlandson, 1810. Before the mausoleum, an exceedingly corpulent gentlemen ("dropsy" refers to fluid accumulation, as can be seen in heart failure) is on his knees suing for the hand of a fashionably cadaverous bachelorette who appears to be in the last stages of wasting away.

of food—fear of typhoid and cholera, for example, contributed to the avoidance of fresh fruits. At best, then, achieving adequate nutrition was no mean feat, but compounded with the foolishness of fashion, it was a near impossibility. Young women took to drinking lemon juice and vinegar as a means of killing their appetite in order to attain the desired paleness. An article in 1824 titled "Beauty Training for Ladies" recommended a diet which prohibited all vegetables except potatoes, as well as butter, cream, milk, cheese, all for the sake of the complexion.[21] Somewhat later, in the heydey of Victorianism, late-nineteenth century women tended to eschew the same foods on moral grounds, believing that foods from animals increased sexual appetites.[22]

21. Burnett, J. (1966), *Plenty and want: A social history of diet in England from 1815 to the present day.* London: Thomas Nelson, pp. 56–57.

22. Bullough, V. & Voght, M. (1973), Women, menstruation, and nineteenth-century medicine, *Bulletin of the History of Medicine, 47,* 66–82.

Thus, the real-life setting in which the sylph emerged in ballet was amidst considerable coughing. *La Sylphide,* the first ballet to reflect the characteristics of the Romantic Period, premiered on March 12, 1832, the title role danced by Marie Taglioni. Significantly, this was one of the first occasions in which a ballerina performed *en pointe* not merely as a technical *tour de force,* but as a means of enhancing the lightness and ethereality, shortening the gap between the mortal and the supernatural. Of course, the masterpiece which still serves as our example of the Romantic Ballet surfaced nine years later with *Giselle,* in which the sylphs were more specifically Willis (spirits of betrothed girls who died after being jilted; they dance their unfaithful lovers to death). The libretto for the ballet was written by none other than Théophile Gautier, himself one of the leaders of the Romantic Movement, who wrote of his youth: "I could not have accepted as a lyrical poet anyone weighing more than ninety-nine pounds."[23]

Not that I am directly blaming Gautier for the current popularity of Tab in dance circles. Nor am I suggesting that Giselle really died of tuberculosis (though maybe she had a touch of it—see Figure 6). I have romped through the weed fields of history only to illustrate that the rich ballet heritage includes a tradition of fashion and beauty that is not exactly robust. That is why I cringe everytime I hear mention of a "classical" ballet body or the "striving for perfection." Perhaps I take these phrases too literally, thinking back on the female of the nineteenth century, slumped on her well-worn couch; for this young lady of good breeding has no obstensible appetite, passes out at the slightest provocation, is as pale as marble, and has a nagging cough. Most likely the ethereal swooner is undernourished, anemic, chronically constipated, and has problems with "the curse."[24] It is taxing to imagine her taking two dance classes a day.

23. Dubos & Dubos, *White plague,* op. cit., p. 247.

24. For additional insight into the health dilemmas of these nineteenth-century maidens, see Hudson, R. P. (1977), The biography of disease: Lessons from chlorosis, *Bulletin of the History of Medicine, 51,* 448–463; Scarlett, E. P. (1965), Doctor out of Zebulun: The vapors, *Archives of Internal Medicine, 116,* 142–146; Vertinsky, P. (1987, Spring), Exercise, physical capability, and the eternally wounded woman in late nineteenth century North America, *Journal of Sports History,* 7–27.

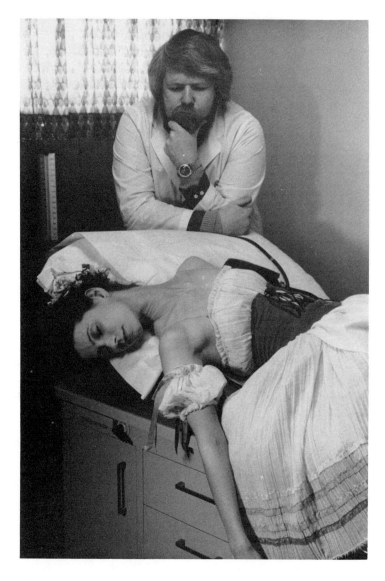

Figure 6. What really did Giselle in? Was it—as commonly believed—a broken heart (secondary to adolescent adjustment reaction/hysterical personality), or did tuberculosis have something to do with it? Medical records are unavailable. (Photo by L. M. Vincent)

From the Ethereal to the Pubertal

While the Romantic Movement brought the ethereal to the ballet in 1832, youth proclaimed itself supreme a century later (one hundred years and one month, to be precise) in the guise of "baby ballerinas." In the autumn of 1931, George Balanchine received an offer from René Blum, then director of the Monte Carlo Theatre, to be the *maître de ballet* of a new company, the Ballets Russes de Monte Carlo. Adamently opposed to rehashing the Ballets Russes of Serge Diaghilev, Balanchine aspired to an entirely new company, a company of extremely youthful dancers in a completely new repertoire. And thus Balanchine set out for Paris to recruit fresh dancing talent, where by chance he ran into old friend Alexandra Danilova, who had heard about plans for the new company and naturally assumed she would figure prominently. To her astonishment, the 27-seven-year old Danilova was informed by Balanchine that she was "much too old" for the kind of company he had in mind.[25]

Indeed she was. At the studios of the two famous Maryinsky ballerinas, Olga Preobrajenska and Mathilde Kschessinska, Balanchine discovered and engaged for his company the teenage trio of Irina Baronova, age 12; Tamara Toumanova, age 13; and Tatiana Riabouchinska, age 14. These three prodigies, all children of Russian émigrés and much too young for leading roles by previously existing standards, nonetheless premiered at the Opéra de Monte Carlo on April 12, 1932. And stars they became, thanks to their remarkable talent, judicious publicity, and a choreographic genius. To me, the emergence and success of the baby ballerinas was a milestone in the evolving, unspoken definition of the ideal on the dance stage.[26]

In fact, the first baby ballerina of renown—though not labeled as such by publicity agents—was really Alicia Markova (the little English girl formerly known as Alice Marks), and once again George Balanchine assumed a pivotal role in ballet history. Although young Alicia had been performing small "suitable" roles in the Diaghilev company, her first major portrayal as the Nightingale in the revival of *Le Chant du Rossignol* came about through Balanchine's intervention. *Le Chant du Rossignol* (with music by Stravinsky and sets by Matisse) premiered in Paris on

25. Taper, B. (1984), *Balanchine: A biography,* New York: Times Books, pp. 135–136; Danilova, A. (1986), *Choura: The memoirs of Alexandra Danilova,* New York: Knopf, pp.117–118.

26. For a comprehensive discussion of the "baby ballerinas" and the Ballet Russes de Monte Carlo in general, see Walker, K. S. (1983), *DeBasil's Ballets Russes,* New York: Atheneum.

Figure 7. A very adolescent-appearing Alicia Markova, as she appeared in *Le Chant du Rossignol (Song of the Nightingale),* the first full-length Balanchine ballet for the Ballets Russes. This baby ballerina "look," which Markova naturally outgrew, is one of the few examples I've come across of a contemporary young ballet body in old photos. (Courtesy of the Dance Collection, The New York Public Library)

June 17, 1925. It was the first full-length ballet to be choreographed by Balanchine for the Ballets Russes, and it was chiefly memorable for the debut of the tiny, frail Markova, whom Balanchine had cast and who was then 15 years old (Figure 7).

Although the baby ballerinas shared the youth and enthusiasm of today's serious ballet student in company schools, from what I can gather from recent conversations with Madame Riabouchinska (now in her seventies, still teaching and running a school in Los Angeles), they did not share the weight obsession. Photographs from the period confirm that they did not share their excessive leanness either. Baronova "always had sexy body," according to Riabouchinska, and Toumanova was certainly not overly thin.

Of the three, Riabouchinska was the thinnest. Cecil Beaton referred to her "thistledown lightness . . . hollow-cheeked face and almost exaggeratedly long legs."[27] Yes, she was "skinny" (her own word); so skinny in fact, that in those early days she wore two pairs of tights for performances and her "mother had to wake me up to feed me at night bread and butter and milk." But Tatiana Riabouchinska was skinny by 1930 standards, not today's, and she was never a dieter (Figure 8). She was particularly fond of macaroni and other pastas, and had acquired a taste for sugar on her spaghetti, hardly Lean Cuisine. She also confirmed, as Baronova has related,[28] that the trio frequented Pasquier, the famous Monte Carlo teashop, where they would have pastry-eating competitions. "We loved pastry," she told me, "and we could afford to eat them." No Sweet 'N Low for these babies.

Competing with the Sylph

Every generation laughs at the old fashions, but follows religiously the new.

Henry David Thoreau

A glance at early photographs of dancers reveals not only how subtly our concept of beauty has crept up on us, but also that one doesn't have

---

27.   Beaton, C. (1951), *Ballet*. New York: Doubleday, p. 41.

28.   According to Taper, *Balanchine*, op. cit., p. 137.

Figure 8. In this photo of Tatiana Riabouchinska (in *Beach,* Ballet Russe de Monte Carlo, Photo: Studio-Iris), we can appreciate a slender, but certainly by no means undernourished, body. (Courtesy of the Dance Collection, The New York Public Library)

Figure 9. Fanny Cerrito as seen through the eyes of an engraver (left) and as seen through the lens of a camera (right). In the former she is light on her feet; in the latter, she is considerably weightier. It appears that a well-placed *jeté* might precipitate a major land-slide . (Reproductions courtesy of the Dance Collection, The New York Public Library at Lincoln Center, Astor, Lenox, and Tilden Foundations)

to be a sylph to portray one. Consider Fanny Cerrito, one of the favorite ballerinas of the 1840s, by comparing her engraved portrait with an actual photograph (Figure 9). In the engraving she is floating in space like a wisp, her repose not initiated by a leap but by a gust of wind, perhaps only a slight draft. Suspended by the buoyancy of the air, she is not merely light, she is weightless.

In the photograph she is considerably weightier. To say she has an abundant bustline and sturdy legs would be downplaying at best. Frankly, one would hate to run into such a substantial frame in a dark studio; she appears as solid as the Chrysler Building and possibly as tough to lift off the ground. In all fairness, this photograph was taken toward the end of her career, when even her contemporaries viewed her as more than ador-ably plump, with a few critics going so far as to hint that she was still a marvelous dancer "in spite of her figure."[29]

29. Miguel, P. (1972), *The ballerinas: From the court of Louis XIV to Pavlova*, New York: Macmillan, p. 216.

But few will dispute that dancers were heavier back then; we need not traverse a century to see the insidious change, to realize that our eyes have been blurred by the deceit of art and fashion. The relatively recent definite trend toward thinness has been ingeniously documented by a survey of Playboy magazine centerfolds and Miss America Pageant participants from 1959 to 1978.[30] Not only were Playboy centerfolds and the Miss America contestants consistently thinner than actuarial norms for comparable women in the general population, but they exhibited a steady decline in their weight in those twenty years. More strikingly, after 1970 the weights of the Miss America pageant finalists were significantly less than the other contestants. Comparing the dancers of the eighties with the more recent past, we note that while the physical demands have become greater, the trend is thinner and thinner, paralleling the society as a whole. Again, this is not to deny the dancer's need to be thin; it is a question of the working definition of "thinness" and the standards by which the criteria are established.

The renowned principal ballerina Alexandra Danilova maintained an "ideal" dancing weight of approximately 112 pounds for her nearly five-foot, five-inch frame throughout a career which lasted for more than three decades. Yet one of her students at the School of American Ballet, considered to have an excellent ballet stature and of roughly the same height and bone structure as Madame Danilova, danced at a weight of 91 pounds. In light of this, it is even more ironic to hear the young woman disparagingly comment on her relative obesity: "You should have seen me at 102," she told me. "I looked awful."

Paradoxically, when you consider the present and past exceptional dancers in ballet, the guidelines of an ideal look have little, if any, meaning whatsoever. It doesn't take particularly astute vision to realize that Cynthia Gregory, Patricia McBride, Martine van Hamel, Merrill Ashley, Melissa Hayden, Suzanne Farrell, or Carla Fracci do not conform to the same, or any particular mold. And many did not consider Judith Jamison to have a dancer's body until they saw her dance. What distinguishes these and other fine dancers from others far transcends height, weight, extension, and bustline. A technically competent dancer with the right look is one thing, but the special dancers are another breed entirely. They are unique, and the sum total of all the intangibles allows them to overcome virtually anything. A New York City ballet instructor observed:

30.   Garner, D. M., Garfinkel, P. E., Schwartz, D., & Thompson, M. (1980), Cultural expectation of thinness of women, *Psychological Reports*, *47*, 483–491.

If you look at the dancers who're around today, or the great artists of the past, very few of them are physically perfect. They all have something wrong; either short arms, short legs, short torso, too big, too tall, wide ears, eyes crossed. There's always something wrong with them somewhere, but they learn to make it work for them. They move so well, and they're so coordinated, that you don't notice that maybe their arms are too short for their body . . . you never really see it.

Mme. Danilova puts it in these terms:

For dancing you have to have talent, and you have to have the look. If you don't have the look, then you have to have double talent. Because your talent makes people forget how you look.

Nonetheless, for the aspiring ballet dancer auditioning for the *corps du ballet,* there may be less latitude as far as individuality is concerned. The premium is on physicality, and often the expectations—either as they are demanded in fact or as they are perceived—might actually be ill-suited for the business of dancing. As one dance instructor put it:

[Some companies] are missing out on a lot of wonderful dancers because they're picking a body type, they're not necessarily picking a talented dancer. And this is where one has to be very, very careful. That you don't just get caught up on someone because of the way they look physically, rather than to take someone who really has a feel for dance, who after careful training and refinement, can maybe lengthen out that sort of square-looking body. It doesn't mean to say because that body isn't long and thin that it shouldn't dance.

The insight and benevolence of this dance instructor was marred somewhat by the following addendum, an attitude which I find quite prevalent among young dancers, and one which is bothersome in its implications:

But if your structure is short and thick—muscular thick—then it has to be *down to the bone,* and if you can get it down to the bone without being ill, fine. If you can't, then you've got to get out of it [dancing].

A seventeen-year-old girl comes to clinic weighing 95 pounds, convinced that something is wrong with her thyroid because she can't lose the "fat" from her muscular thighs. A fifteen-year-old girl who resembles a curtain rod is on a liquid protein regimen for weight control, under the supervision of a physician and with the consent and encouragement of her stage mother. A five-foot, three-inch tall ballet-scholarship student, barely tipping the scale at 100 pounds, wants dietary advice on how to reduce her weight to 85 pounds in two weeks for an audition.

Obviously it is easier for some people to conform to a given look than others, and in the case of the élite ballerina, more than one "selection" process will determine her ultimate career survival. But the competition is always relative, usually needless, often futile, and perhaps self-destructive—be it the short, compact dancer competing with the long, thin one, or the long, thin one competing with the sylph. Preoccupation with weight, when the expectations are unrealistic, amounts to an ominous distortion.

2 Metabolic Illusion versus Reality

To preserve one's health by too strict a regimen is in itself a tedious malady.

François, duc de la Rochefoucauld

So convenient a thing it is to be a reasonable creature since it enables one to find or make a reason for every thing one has a mind to do.

Benjamin Franklin

The Duped Dancer

Often I espy particularly unhealthy-looking patrons coming from or going into health food stores. Not wishing to belittle these establishments, I only want to point out that: (1) healthy foods don't necessarily have to be "health foods"; and (2) concern with eating does not insure proper eating. Consumers may be victimized by oddball diets, misleading product promotion, or outright fake food cures. Sir William Osler noted that "the greater the ignorance, the greater the dogmatism," and in the business of nutrition, a little ignorance can go a long way.[1] Dancers and other athletes, often looking for something to give them an edge, competitive or otherwise, are especially vulnerable to being duped. Granted, compared to hard work and training, a nutritional magic wand would be an easy way out.

A New York physician analyzed this peculiar blind spot, remarking that dancers:

> . . . are so involved in their bodies, and the minute changes that happen to their bodies, that they are willing to listen to anything. Anything that ranges from utter nonsense to sense, but they have no standard of judgment. . . . It's their bodies, and how they perform; there's nothing else in their lives, and they know it. And here you are—this sort of normal person interviewing them—and how can they tell you about the fanaticism? I mean, they're embarrassed.

Up to a point, and with a cynical eye on nutritional history, food fallacies may not have dire consequences and may be appreciated simply for their own sake. For example, when ordering a sandwich on whole wheat, I am mindful of a great tradition. Hippocrates would no doubt have made the same choice, as he recommended unbolted wheat-meal for its "salutary effect upon the bowels." The Greek wrestlers ate a coarse dark bread, and, according to Pliny, the Romans subsisted on it in the days of their greatest glory. Nibbling on the crust, I recall that the Emperor Augustus did the same while bouncing about in his chariot seeking new worlds to conquer, as did Seneca (he stressed eating bread in the standing position, however). For even more reassurance, I think back on Sylvester Graham, who promised his generation that they would all live to be a hundred if they ate brown bread. In brief, even if it's a dry sandwich on stale whole wheat toast, I can still feel pretty exhilarated about every mouthful.

On the other hand, if I happen to select white bread (drawing dirty, condescending glances or comments from ardently health-conscious eaters), I rationalize that it is vitamin fortified, that I probably have an adequate fiber content in my diet from other foods, that my digestive juices really get into gear for foods I find palatable, and finally, that

---

1. Surveys have documented that, as a group, dancers know little about basic nutrition. For instance, many do not know the four basic food groups, or that carbohydrates are the best source of energy, or that vitamins cannot be used as an energy source.

Sylvester Graham—despite the fact he was famous enough to have a cracker named after him—wasn't all that reliable. In addition to pushing brown bread with incredible zeal, he claimed that condiments caused the blues and led to insanity, tea produced delirium tremens, eating meat inflamed the "baser propensities," and both chicken pie and lewdness caused cholera.[2] To further dampen his credibility, Sylvester died at the age of fifty-seven.

"Too strict a regimen" and wholesale acceptance of food fads can lead to any number of pitfalls. Excerpts from an interview with a young ballet student who was very concerned about eating "properly" in order to help her dancing as well as maintain her weight are quite illustrative:

> *Dancer:* I've tried everything. Like the pineapple diet. For two days I ate nothing but fresh pineapple.
> *Vincent:* Why did you quit?
> *Dancer:* Because it hurt my tongue [laughter]; and you're only suppose to go on it for two days because after that you get weak. And then I got really sick and had to see a doctor because I was just eating vegetables [gastrointestinal complaints].
> *Vincent:* When did you do this?
> *Dancer:* For the next four days after the pineapple . . . then I got sick. Also I was just taking liquids on the week-ends . . . I figured it didn't matter if I was weak on the weekends, just as long as I ate protein and stuff during the week [for classes].
> *Vincent:* What kind of liquids?
> *Dancer:* I'd have carrot juice (and maybe I'd eat a carrot), but mostly juices; orange juice or something like that.
> *Vincent:* All weekend?
> *Dancer:* . . . and coffee, tea, diet soda, and lots of water.
> *Vincent:* [Specifying needlessly] Coffee with Sweet 'N Low.
> *Dancer:* Oh, yeah.
> *Vincent:* How did you feel?
> *Dancer:* I felt very loose on Monday.
> *Vincent:* How was your endurance?
> *Dancer:* Well, I could never really tell the difference between being weak from not eating and exhausted from not getting enough sleep.

The dancer revealed that at the time of her dietary indiscretions, she was working outside of dance four nights a week—getting home at about 11 P.M.—dancing four to six hours a day, and getting up at 6 A.M. to

2. Carson, G. (1957), *Cornflake crusade*, New York: Rinehart, p. 50. For additional commentary on Sylvester Graham, see Schwartz, H. (1986), *Never satisfied*, New York: Free Press.

complete correspondence work for her high-school equivalency. After the pineapple-vegetable-liquid regimen had met with less that positive results, the dancer embarked on a low carbohydrate diet—occasionally "splurging" on a grapefruit—for about three weeks.

> *Vincent:* But you're aware that you need carbohydrates for energy?
> *Dancer:* Yeah, I found that out.
> *Vincent:* How?
> *Dancer:* Getting spaced-out all the time. I didn't have enough energy . . . I know that I could pretty much eat what I want to, three meals a day, basically fifteen hundred or maybe two thousand calories a day, and I might be five or seven pounds heavier than I am now, and maintain that without any problem.
> *Vincent:* So you think that the weight you want to attain for ballet may be unnatural for you?
> *Dancer:* It is.
> *Vincent:* So why? Why do you go through all this business?
> *Dancer:* Because I want to be good.
> *Vincent:* I see. [Heavy sigh]

Food faddism may be financially costly, may cause the dancer to credit satisfaction and success to other things besides talent and hard work, and may also inhibit the development of optimum performing capabilities. Unnecessary measures need not be hazardous in themselves to be detrimental; taken to extremes, they may exclude healthful practices and be harmful indirectly. For instance, fatigue precipitated by inadequate nutritional reserves might make one more susceptible to a musculoskeletal injury, assuredly a more tangible problem than the loss of pep from which it resulted.

Faddist tendencies aside, emphasis on slimness in itself may result in miserable eating habits. One professional ballet dancer treated her dietary intake with characteristic abandon:

> *Vincent:* What did you eat yesterday?
> *Dancer:* I had a bowel of onion soup and some bread.
> *Vincent:* All day?
> *Dancer:* Yeah, and some coffee. [Laughter] About three cups of coffee. But I'm going to start eating more.
> *Vincent:* What did you eat the day before?
> *Dancer:* I don't know; I don't think I ate. Oh, I had some yogurt.
> *Vincent:* All day?
> *Dancer:* Yes, and some coffee.

Vincent: With sugar?
Dancer: Sweet 'N Low.

It invariably boils down to misplaced priorities. The conscientious eater may be conscientious about everything except eating; never skimping on daily vitamins (sometimes in megadoses) or supplements such as lecithin, dolomite, wheat germ, and the like, but somehow forgetting that energy is derived from *food.* The end result may be a suboptimal nutritional state with a vitamin-enriched urine (most vitamin excesses are rapidly excreted by the kidney, particularly the water-soluble B and C vitamins). The dancer quoted above was somewhat shocked to learn that her interviewer occasionally indulged in "regular" cola, as she was quite concerned about avoiding junk calories. Without question, purified sugars are much too large a component of the daily caloric intake of the average American (and have been implicated in the causation of conditions such as obesity, diabetes, and coronary artery disease), but in light of her own dietary regimen, a few "junk" calories would have been better than no calories at all.

Counting calories

So how many calories[3] do dancers consume, anyway? A lot fewer than some of us might expect, according to a number of reliable nutritional surveys. Drs. Cohen et al.,[4] analyzing six-day food diaries of ten female American Ballet Theatre dancers, found a median daily caloric intake of only 1,588 kcal (range, 977–2,361 kcal).[5] Six of the ten women fell below the Recommended Daily Allowance (RDA) for reference women

---

3. A "calorie" is defined as the amount of heat energy necessary to raise the temperature of a gram of water from 15 to 16°C. Since this is a very small amount, calorie counters actually keep track of "kilocalories" (the amount of energy required to raise one kilogram of water by 1°). Since I have chosen to employ common usage, "calorie" and "kilocalorie" (kcal) will be used interchangeably.

4. Cohen, J. L., Potosnak, L., Frank, O., & Baker, H. (1985), A nutritional and hematologic assessment of elite ballet dancers, *Physician and Sportsmedicine, 13*, 43–54.

5. A quick statistical refresher: "Mean" is synonymous with "average," and is derived by dividing the sum of a set of terms by the number of such terms. "Median" refers to the midpoint location, the number in an ordered set below and above which there is an equal number of values. In general, the mean and median are different because the median is less influenced by extreme values within the set. For example, the mean of 1, 2, 3, 3, 10 is 1 + 2 + 3 + 3 + 10 divided by 5, or 3.6; the median is 3, the middle number in the sequence.

of similar age, weight, and height.[6] Hamilton et al.,[7] in a twenty-four-hour survey of nineteen professional female dancers from four classical ballet companies, found a median caloric intake of 1,694 kcal (range 650–3,758 kcal). Eleven of these women were eating less than 85 percent of the RDA; four less than 66 percent of the RDA; and two less than 50 percent of the RDA. Calabrese et al.,[8] analyzing three-day food records during a typical rehearsal week of twenty-five female members of the Cleveland Ballet, determined that mean caloric intake of these regional dancers was an even more spartan 1,358 kcal daily (range, 550–2,115 kcal). Seventy-six percent of these women ingested less than 85 percent of the RDA; 40 percent less than 66 percent of the RDA; and 20 percent, less than half of the RDA.

A West Coast study of ninety-two adolescent dancers enrolled in six professional schools yielded comparable results. Using three-day diet histories, Benson et al.[9] found that average daily caloric intake was 1,890 kcal. However, nearly half of these student dancers consumed less than 1,800 kcal per day, 28.9 percent consumed less than 1,500 per day, and 10.8 percent consumed less than 1,200 daily. In my experience with adolescents in ballet company schools in New York City, even these figures seem high. This impression was substantiated by a survey of the caloric intake of Joffrey Ballet School students, part of a psychological study by Druss and Silverman.[10] Although the data must be judged as more subject to inaccuracies than these other studies (since caloric intake was self-reported on questionnaires, not by a nutritionist analyzing a food log), the results are nonetheless telling. The average daily estimated intake of thirty-one respondents was 1,000 kcal (range, 400–1,900), with two-thirds of these girls claiming to consume 1,000 calories per day or less.

To make matters worse, the low-calorie diets typically are of low

6. Keep in mind that such caloric norms apply to the general population of women, not just highly active ones like professional athletes and dancers.

7. Hamilton, L. H., Brooks-Gunn, J., & Warren, M. P. (1986), Nutritional intake of female dancers: A reflection of eating problems, *International Journal of Eating Disorders, 5,* 925–934.

8. Calabrese, L. H., Kirkendall, D. T., Floyd, M., et al. (1983), Menstrual abnormalities, nutritional patterns, and body composition in female classical ballet dancers, *Physician and Sportsmedicine, 11,* 86–98.

9. Benson, J., Gillien, D. M., Bourdet, K., & Loosli, A. R. (1985), Inadequate nutrition and chronic calorie restriction in adolescent ballerinas, *Physician and Sportsmedicine, 13,* 79–90.

10. Druss, R. G. & Silverman, J. A. (1979), Body image and perfectionism of ballerinas: Comparison and contrast with anorexia nervosa, *General Hospital Psychiatry, 2,* 115–121.

nutritional density and unbalanced, the distribution of nutrients favoring excessive protein at the expense of carbohydrates. (A balanced diet should be comprised of 10–15 percent of total calories as protein, 50–60 percent as carbohydrate, and 30–35 percent as fat.) Documented vitamin and mineral deficiencies in dancers include those of iron and Vitamin B12 (due to avoidance of red meat), calcium and Vitamin D (inadequate milk consumption), and thiamine, folic acid, niacin, pantothenic acid, biotin, and Vitamin B6 (from not enough dietary variation).[11] And although a high percentage of dancers take supplements (between 40 to more than 90 percent), vitamin and mineral deficiencies are not necessarily completely corrected.

Since the estimated calories needed by a female dancer is in the range of 2,000 to 2,200 per day (this figure will vary according to body size and age, young dancers during rapid growth requiring more), it doesn't take an accountant to figure out that the ledger sheet here just doesn't balance. If more energy is going out than coming in (and if the First Law of Thermodynamics[12] is worth its salt), then why don't dancers undergo progressive weight loss and melt away? The answer is threefold: (1) dancers don't expend as much energy as they might appear to; (2) a variety of ongoing physiological adaptations are at work, enabling the body to get the most (and the best) mileage per calorie; and (3) caloric intake over the short term may not accurately reflect total caloric intake because of the relatively high incidence of food binges.

Let's review some basic physiology and then consider these explanations one at a time.

A lesson in metabolism and energy demands of dancers

Perhaps someone should hire a large public-relations firm to spruce up the image of "fat," the victim of a pervasive smear campaign. In common usage, we tend to think of fat as synonymous with obesity. This imprecision (which I am guilty of in this book) not only simplifies, but implicitly distorts. Obesity, without question, may be detrimental to good health. Shorter life expectancy, higher incidence of diseases such as hypertension, heart disease, and diabetes have a recognized relationship to obesity, public awareness of which has no doubt contributed to our

---

11.   Cohen et al., A nutritional and hematologic assessment, op. cit.

12.   "Matter is neither created nor destroyed, but converted from one form to another."

culture's craving for slimness. But the negative aspects of an overabundance of fat have overshadowed the physiological importance of normal amounts. That an ounce of fat should be viewed as a near-abomination exemplifies the irrationality and blind hatred directed toward our own distortion. In essence, we have become dietary McCarthyites, with fat filling in for the communists.

In the human being, fat is the principal stored form of energy, accounting for approximately 80–85 percent of body fuel stores in the average man. This is a practical arrangement, since "lipid" (the highbrow designation for fat) is stored with very little water. "Glycogen" (the storage form of carbohydrate) and protein, on the other hand, are present in the body in association with water (the ratio of water to protein and glycogen is in the neighborhood of three or four to one). Thus, if a man's primary energy reservoirs were relegated to protein and glycogen, he would be so bogged down with excess obligatory water weight that something as basic as moving would be quite an accomplishment.[13]

Lipid synthesis and storage is, in fact, a prerequisite to survival in any species that depends on motility. Not surprisingly, fat storage is most prominent in migratory insects and birds, as well as in seeds, pollens, fruits, and nuts (the last relying on passive mobility for propagation of the species). This contrasts with carbohydrate as the major energy form in most of the plant kingdom (which may be one of many reasons that plants don't creep off the windowsill at night or watermelons have never been observed flying). Through painstaking evolution, human metabolic processes have been selected which result in fat storage during periods of plenty (after the back-up, emergency reserves of liver and muscle glycogen have been filled), and fat depletion during leaner times. Protein may be called upon to stoke the metabolic fire, but it is preferentially spared as fuel by the body so it can fulfill its numerous other functions (as enzyme, contractile, or structural protein). Energy, then, is obtained from fat stores (in the form of free fatty acids) or from carbohydrate (in the form of liver glycogen, muscle glycogen, or circulating blood glucose); the relative contribution of each source is variable and determined by nutritional status and the amount (duration and intensity) of activity.

For intensive work of short duration, the glycogen stored in muscle is the most efficient energy source (we might view all-out physical activity as an "emergency" situation in Nature's eyes, because the energy burst

---

13.   For a review of energy storage and use as it relates to fasting, see Cahill, G. F., Jr. (1970), Starvation in man, *New England Journal of Medicine, 282,* 668–675.

required of a sprinter is not much different than the fuel needed by a primitive human being pursued by a fleet and hungry animal). During this burst-type activity, energy is extracted from glycogen by processes that require no oxygen—"anaerobic" metabolism. The use of this metabolic pathway is not only limited by the amount of glycogen available, but also by the breakdown product, lactic acid, which accumulates in the muscle faster than it can be dissipated and impairs muscle function. The Bluebird Variation from *The Sleeping Beauty*, for example, one of the most intense and demanding pieces in the classical repertory, lasts only about 45 seconds. One would strain to imagine work of this speed and intensity persisting for another minute nonstop, let alone 15 or 20. Even the best-trained physical specimen can only go so far; at some point, the dancer's complexion might change to the color of his costume; he would be too pooped to execute another *brisé volé*. The depletion of muscle glycogen by anaerobic metabolism is associated with exhaustion.

Glycogen stores are protected by intermittent exercise, short periods of rest, or work of less intensity, which allows other fuels to assume more of the burden. In longer-term exercise (which does not require maximal effort from the muscle, but rather a submaximal effort for a sustained period of time), the breakdown of nutrients—mainly glucose and fats—occurs in the presence of oxygen via the aerobic pathway. Aerobic work is limited not by fatigue-producing end-products (with oxygen available, nutrients are completely broken down to carbon dioxide and water), but by the rate at which oxygen can be delivered to the active tissues by the heart and lungs. "Aerobic exercises" are those that push muscles to work moderately but long enough to shift the balance from a relatively heavy dependence on glycogen to a predominant dependence on fatty acids.[14]

While anaerobic metabolism can use only glucose (in the form of glycogen) as the source of energy, aerobic pathways can utilize all three foodstuffs in varying relative amounts. In the resting state, muscles depend almost entirely on the oxidation of fatty acids. With exercise of low intensity, glucose becomes an increasingly important source of energy. The use of free fatty acids again predominates in prolonged mild exercise

14. According to the American College of Sports Medicine, exercise training should consist of 15 to 60 minutes of continuous aerobic activity at an intensity of 60–90 percent of maximum heart rate or 50–85 percent of maximum oxygen uptake, three to five days per week. See: ACSM (1978), The recommended quantity and quality of exercise for developing and maintaining fitness in healthy adults, *Medicine and Science in Sports and Exercise, 10*, vii–x.

(the relative contribution of fat becomes roughly twice that of carbohydrate).[15]

Although the body makes every effort to conserve its protein, when this is no longer possible, amino acids—the basic components of protein—may be drafted into picking up some of the slack and aiding as a source of fuel (after first being converted into glucose). In this instance, the body allows the greatest possible leeway through the establishment of its priorities. While low levels of insulin ultimately will instigate the breakdown of protein and its mobilization as fuel, exercise counteracts this effect. Muscle contraction in itself inhibits protein breakdown and stimulates protein synthesis—the long-term effect of repeated muscular work being muscle buildup ("hypertrophy"), not wasting. So in the dancer who is not eating well, if protein breakdown is to occur, it will occur preferentially from the muscles that are not being worked, which is why dancers may be quite bony in the chest and arms and still maintain well-delineated, hypertrophied leg musculature.

In general, though, how does dancing stack up as an energy-demanding activity? Researchers have been able to characterize the energy demands of ballet dancers specifically by directly measuring their oxygen consumption (see Figure 10) as well as by monitoring the heart rate's response to dancing.[16] The results reflect two characteristics of ballet training and performing: (1) ballet is a "mixed" type of exercise, with a strong static component (placement, posing, balancing) along with the more dynamic component (traveling, turning, jumping); (2) significant intervals of rest punctuate very intensive combinations (this is especially true when performing).

Thus, classical ballet is not aerobic in nature, and ballet dancers, although possessing a higher-than-average heart and lung capacity, are nonetheless best classified as "nonendurance" athletes. The bottom line is that classical ballet does not share the high-energy expenditure of many

---

15. Felig, P. & Wahren, J. (1975), Fuel homeostasis in exercise, *New England Journal of Medicine, 293*, 1078–1084.

16. See Cohen, J. L., Segal, K. R., & McArdle, W. D. (1982), Heart rate response to ballet stage performance, *Physician and Sportsmedicine, 10*, 120–133; Cohen, J. L., Segal, K. R., Witriol, I., & McArdle, W. D. (1982), Cardiorespiratory responses to ballet exercise and the VO_{2max} of elite ballet dancers, *Medicine and Science in Sports and Exercise, 14*, 212–217; Mostardi, R. A., Porterfield, J. A., Greenberg, B., et al. (1983), Musculoskeletal and cardiopulmonary characteristics of the professional ballet dancer, *Physician and Sportsmedicine, 11*, 53–61; Schantz, P. G. & Astrand, P.-O. (1984), Physiological characteristics of classical ballet, *Medicine and Science in Sports and Exercise, 16*, 472–476.

Figure 10. No, this isn't a new costume concept for the Scotch Symphony. Illustrated is an American Ballet Theatre dancer performing an allegro exercise while breathing into a meteorological balloon and equipment used to determine metabolic data under actual classroom conditions. (I assume no partnered lifts were attempted.) (Photo courtesy of Jerald L. Cohen, M.D., reprinted with permission from Cohen, J.L., Segal, K.R., Witriol, I. & McArdle, W.D. (1982), Cardiorespiratory responses to ballet exercise and the VO_{2max} of elite ballet dancers, *Medicine and Science in Sports and Exercise, 14,* 212–217 Copyright © by American College of Sports Medicine)

other athletic pursuits (such as jogging, swimming, or even figure skating).[17] In fact, the estimated net caloric output in a standard one-hour ballet class (twenty-eight minutes of *barre,* thirty-two minutes of center work) averages only 200 kcal for women.[18] In comparison, a distance runner could easily expend twice the calories per unit of body weight.[19] This all translates into bad dietary news for the dancer, who is expected to maintain ultra-leanness without the benefit of a discipline that provides for a generous expenditure of calories.

There is even a price to be paid for expertise, since training by itself makes one a more efficient energy machine. Consider a principal ballerina doing a series of combinations across a studio floor next to a less-trained and less-skilled counterpart (they may both be the same height, weight, age, have the exact body type, or even be identical twins, if you will). The latter dancer, not as smooth or as proficient at execution, must exert more effort to accomplish the steps and maintain balance; she is working harder and using more energy (burning more calories) than the accomplished dancer. But to begin with, since the number of calories required by an individual depends on the amount of body tissue needed to be maintained, a 95-pound female ballet dancer will obviously be able to get by on fewer calories than a 170-pound male. Thus, not only may a dancer require relatively few calories because of diminutive size and the nonendurance nature of ballet; skill may further minimize her energy expenditure.

The law of diminishing returns

And here the plot fattens. Classic studies of prolonged caloric restriction have shown that fasting subjects have a decreased metabolic rate, exhibit a voluntary decrease in the amount of physical activity undertaken, and derive a greater percentage of energy from available fat depots (conserving body protein and water). In short, during nutritional hard times, the body establishes priorities, slowing down its furnace and becoming quite miserly in order to get the most out of the available energy. Despite its innate wisdom, however, the body is not savvy enough to appreciate the difference between a weight-reducing diet and starvation.

---

17.   For an excellent review of the physiological aspects of dance, particularly in comparison with other sports, see Kirkendall, D. T. & Calabrese, L. H. (1983), Physiological aspects of dance, *Clinics in Sports Medicine, 2,* 525–537.

18.   Cohen et al., Cardiorespiratory responses, op. cit.

19.   Kirkendall, D. T. & Calabrese, L. H., Physiological aspects of dance, op. cit.

According to the widely accepted "setpoint" theory, individuals (without their knowing it) vigorously and effectively defend a particular body weight by means of a built-in control system dictating how much fat one should carry.[20] One way for the body to counteract being displaced from its own ideal weight (in either direction) is to adjust its internal rate of energy expenditure. For example, a "successful" diet may promote alterations in metabolism which significantly reduce the number of calories subsequently needed to maintain the status quo (this also implies, unfortunately for the dieter, that a return to normal levels of food intake can quickly lead to weight gain).

Not only dieting, but exercise training alone may also precipitate these unseen adaptations.[21] Factors potentially mediating a diminished expenditure of internal energy include decreased metabolic rate; lower diet-induced "thermogenesis" (less energy is needed for digesting and storing nutrients); increased efficiency of food utilization; diminished thyroid gland function; and changes in the activity of adipose tissue.[22] Obviously, a dieting female may be doubly prone to provoking this protective response to energy restriction. The female dancer, by her eating habits and training regimen, may thus perpetuate her own personal energy crisis by forcing her body to pick up the slack.

20. For an excellent academic review of setpoint theory, see Keesey, R. E. (1980), A setpoint analysis of the regulation of body weight, in Stunkard, A. J. (ed.), *Obesity*, Philadelphia: W. B. Saunders, pp. 144–165. The general reader might do better by consulting Bennett, W. & Gurin, J. (1982), *The dieter's dilemma: Eating less and weighing more*, New York: Basic Books, pp. 60–87. And while you're at it, read the whole book. The *Dieter's dilemma* is an excellent introduction to this material (and much more), and is the one diet book that every dieter should read.

21. Tremblay, A., Després, J.-P., & Bouchard, C. (1985), The effects of exercise-training on energy balance and adipose tissue morphology and metabolism, *Sports Medicine, 2*, 223–233.

22. Tremblay, A., Côté, J., & LeBlanc, J. (1983), Diminished dietary thermogenesis in exercise-trained human subjects, *European Journal of Applied Physiology, 52*, 1–4; Boyden, T. W., Pamenter, R. W., Stanforth, P., et al. (1982), Evidence for mild thyroidal impairment in women undergoing endurance training, *Journal of Clinical Endocrinology and Metabolism, 54*, 53–56; and Brownell, K. D., Steen, S. N., & Wilmore, J. H. (1987), Weight regulation practices in athletes: Analysis of metabolic and health effects, *Medicine and Science in Sports and Exercise, 19*, 546–556.

"Pigging-Out"

The thing I've noticed most of all, is that they [dancers] eat in excess; it's either one or the other. Instead of cutting down their food generally if they're trying to lose weight, they just cut everything out. And then they go from one extreme to the other; they're starving one day and they're gorging the next day.

Ballet Instructor, New York City

Dietary willpower comes easily to few of us, but most nondancers won't ever be called upon to submit to the degree of dietary denial and discipline that is for some dancers a matter of course. Yet female dancers' eating patterns rarely stay on an even keel. Carbohydrate denial goes on for only so long before a barely discernable crack appears in the resolve. Then comes the binge. Resolve shattering like glass, the dancer succumbs to the likes of chocolate bars (Tobler Mocha), chocolate-chip cookies (Entennman's), and ice cream (Häagan-Daz's rum raisin). To use the vernacular, "pigging out" is a conspicuous facet of the dance subculture.

In the study of the Cleveland Ballet Company cited earlier, moderate food "binging" was documented in 70 percent of the dancers[23] (recall that the three-day food survey of the women in this group revealed an average daily caloric intake of 1,358 kcal, a figure clearly not representative of binging days, which are more likely to occur on the weekends). Binge eating was predictably even more prevalent in a younger group of serious dancers (45 females, ages 12–21, in a professional ballet school): 86.7 percent.[24]

Perhaps a definition of terms is needed, as one person's dessert might be another's pig-out. There is a considerable range between such a dietary indiscretion as cake à la mode and a condition known as "bulimia," compulsive eating of an extreme degree, usually followed by vomiting (bulimia will be discussed in more detail in chapter 3). Because of this subjective variability, I routinely asked ballet students to specify their "best" or "biggest pig-outs." Representative samples included:

23.   Calabrese, L. H., et al., Menstrual abnormalities, op. cit.

24.   Braisted, J. R., Mellin, L., Gong, E. J., & Irwin, C. E., Jr. (1985), The adolescent ballet dancer: Nutritional practices and characteristics associated with anorexia nervosa, *Journal of Adolescent Health Care, 6,* 365–371.

- A full dinner, followed by ice cream and one-third of a cheese-cake.
- Bagel and cream cheese, a pint of ice cream, licorice candy, several cookies, and a chocolate bar.
- Two pints of ice cream and a piece of baklava (followed by Ex-Lax).
- A piece of pizza, half a blueberry cheesecake, half a package of Vienna lady fingers, half a bar of halvah, and a toasted English muffin (with butter).

Now, as legend has it, the Greek Olympic wrestling champion, Milo of Croton, once carried a four-year-old bull around an athletic stadium, killed it with a single blow, and ate it in one day. But whether or not this historical pig-out is exaggerated, we must keep in mind that Milo was big, bad, and mean. The weight of the dancers whose indulgences I cite ranges between 100 and 125 pounds, certainly not in the wrestler's weight division.

For young dancers, pigging-out may be a social occasion—another example of the food-oriented direction that the cloistered milieu can take. In the words of a fledgling ballet-company member, describing the antics of her cohorts residing in a women's residence hall:

> Everybody gets together and plans a day when they're going to buy everything they like to eat—all kinds of junk—and just eat and eat and eat it all. More or less it's just a party, but for us it's a pig-out, because we aren't supposed to do it.

The aftermath of the pig-out may be feelings of shame, guilt, anger, resignation, or depression; but whatever the reaction, amends can be made by subsequently stepping up dieting measures or—what is sometimes seen as more convenient and immediate expiation—self-induced vomiting or a bout of laxatives. Dancers themselves generally blame this type of eating on a number of factors, such as their general preoccupation with food or on moods (frustration, boredom, the blues, disappointment at failing to get a part). What is more likely, however, is that binging is a reaction to dieting itself. Even naturally thin dancers may be functioning at a weight below their "setpoint," and there is a stressful price to pay.

Individuals who consistently resist the urge to eat have been termed "restrained" eaters.[25] Psychologists, gauging dieting behavior and sepa-

25. Herman, C. P, & Polivy, J. (1980), Restrained eating, in Stunkard, A. J. (ed.), *Obesity,* op. cit., pp. 208–225; Herman, C. P. & Polivy, J. (1975), Anxiety, restraint, and eating behavior,

rating subjects into "restrained" and "unrestrained" categories by questionnaire (the "restraint scale"), have concluded that restraint is a major determinant of eating behavior. Women are more likely to be restrained eaters than men, and restrained eating subjects of both sexes experience more craving for food and have more eating binges than unrestrained eaters.[26] Dietary restraint involves a conscious attempt to deny physiology, an effort of will.[27] Can there be a more conspicuous group of restrained eaters than dancers? Hard to imagine. Well, then, what is the nature of their potential physiological adversaries?

Researchers studying the extreme starvation of anorexia nervosa have noted that the severe carbohydrate restriction of these patients results in an abnormal insulin response to carbohydrate ingestion (high levels of insulin are sustained for longer periods than would be expected). It has been suggested that in these cases the abnormal response triggered by a small amount of carbohydrates leads to a compelling need to continue eating carbohydrates.[28] In other words, abstinence from carbohydrates might lead to a greater dependency on carbohydrates and to cravings that precipitate a binge.

But "adipose tissue" (yet another highbrow designation for fat) may actually be the major opponent here. Researchers have also established that body weight is determined both by the number of fat cells in the body and the average size or weight of these fat cells.[29] Fat reduction induced by both exercise training and dieting appears to be solely attributable to a reduction in the size of fat cells, since once formed, fat cells

Journal of Abnormal Psychology, 84, 666–672; Stunkard, A. J. (1981), "Restrained eating": What it is and a new scale to measure it, in Cioffi, L. A., James, W. P. T., & van Itallie, T. B. (eds.), *The body weight regulatory system: Normal and disturbed mechanisms,* New York: Raven Press, pp. 243–251; Stunkard, A. J. & Messick, S. (1985), The three-factor eating questionnaire to measure dietary restraint, disinhibition, and hunger, *Journal of Psychosomatic Research, 29,* 71–83.

26.   Wardle, J. (1980), Dietary restraint and binge eating, *Behavioural Analysis and Modification, 4,* 201–209.

27.   The concept of eating restraint, although compatible with the setpoint hypothesis, is not dependent upon the actual existence of a setpoint. Setpoint or not, dieting creates a pressure to eat, and restrained eaters suffer from frustration, with binges occurring when frustration mounts to intolerable levels.

28.   Crisp, A. H. (1967), The possible significance of some behavioral correlates of weight and carbohydrate intake, *Journal of Psychosomatic Research, 11,* 117–131.

29.   Sjöström, L. (1980), Fat cells and body weight, in Stunkard, A. J. (ed.), *Obesity,* op. cit.; Björntorp, P., Development of adipose tissue, in L. A. Cioffi et al. (eds.), *Body weight regulatory system,* op. cit., pp. 353–360. Again, Bennett & Gurin's *The dieter's dilemma,* op. cit., provides a superb review of this subject.

evidently become lifelong companions. Dieters with "skinny" fat cells are likely to be below their "natural" weight, and as you might suspect, they are also likely to qualify for the restrained-eater category.

Without doubt, the aesthetic demands of dance have placed a significant proportion of dancers squarely into the jaws of a biological trap. The dogged insistence on ultra-leanness eventuates in a physiological siege mentality, with will power clashing against biological needs. The inevitable end result is a suboptimal diet, suboptimal energy reserves, continual dietary stress and frustration, and virtually no feasible escape from this self-excavated metabolic rut.

Misattribution: Justifying the Means

Once priorities have been misplaced, or an erroneous premise is accepted, bad habits or fallacies may be perpetuated through "misattribution," the attributing of a symptom to an incorrect cause. Take the dancer who lacks pep in her last class of the day. Perhaps she will blame "hypoglycemia," failure to take enough B vitamins, brewer's yeast, or Tiger's Milk. By some twisted logic, the fact that she has had only a cup of coffee and some yogurt for sustenance while dancing six hours will not be perceived as a likely, or even possible, cause. Another dancer may blame her inability to lose weight on a metabolic derangement or on hypothyroidism, discounting late-night cookie binges or her insistence on taking several Energol tablets every day (Vitamin E in the form of wheat-germ oil, with 60 calories concentrated in every capsule). And a young dancer may misattribute the dancing prowess of a contemporary to her diet of popcorn, Tab, and liquid protein, overlooking superior talent, discipline, and training, and failing to comprehend that the dancer performs well not because of her diet, but in spite of it.

Misattribution in part stems from a confusing aspect of medical science: many ailments, major and minor, are heralded by symptoms which are the same, or relatively nonspecific. Additionally, false symptoms (normal physiological conditions such as low spirits, tiredness, tension, mild insomnia, and the like) may be mistaken for real symptoms. And since much of our interpretation of symptoms has a psychological component, we cannot always trust our perceptions of our own experience. It might still be argued that if one feels better with a particular offbeat regimen or unorthodox dietary manipulation—whether owing to a

placebo effect or to an unknown or unsubstantiated biochemical altera-
tion—then the regimen has some positive worth; that is, provided the
regimen is not directly harmful in itself, or indirectly so in fostering a
concomitant neglect of overall good health. Dietary idiosyncrasies may
be viewed benevolently as long as they aren't idiocies. Since an awareness of a smidgen more physiology may help to demarcate the difference,
let's review some basics of fuel management and transformation and how
they relate to the self-diagnosed, self-confessed hypoglycemic.

Hypoglycemia: Taking the Rap

Since the maintenance of a blood glucose level within certain limits is
of high priority to the body (the major consumer of glucose is the brain,
using roughly a fifth of the body's calories at rest), fine hormonal regulation is crucial, and the hormone insulin plays a major role (Figure 11).
Cells in the pancreas (called *"beta cells"*) constantly monitor blood sugar
levels and release insulin accordingly. A slight rise in sugar levels, such
as occurs after a meal, augments insulin production. Relatively high
levels of this hormone open up the body cells for the storage of fuel,
removing the excess sugar (and other nutrients) from the bloodstream to
bring the levels back to normal. In hungry states or with exercise—when
glucose supplies in the circulating pool begin to dwindle—low levels of
insulin initiate the mobilization of fuels from storage, again to keep the
glucose levels within a desirable range.[30]
  If insulin is the principal fuel coordinator, the major energy transformer in the body is the liver (Figure 12), normally the sole site of
production and release of glucose into the bloodstream (muscles lack the
capability to convert glycogen into glucose for release into the blood, so
muscle carbohydrate stores in one area are of little use for muscles elsewhere in the body). The liver can provide glucose in two ways: (1) from
the breakdown of its own glycogen stores (a process called *"glycogenolysis"*); or (2) the production of glucose de novo from glycerol, lactate,
pyruvate, and certain amino acids (a process called *"gluconeogenesis"*).
Simply then, the fed state is characterized by high levels of insulin which
instigate storage by the liver (a cessation of new glucose production and

30. For an excellent and more comprehensive review of the physiology of insulin, see Cahill, G.
F., Jr. (1971), Physiology of insulin in man, *Diabetes, 20,* 785–799.

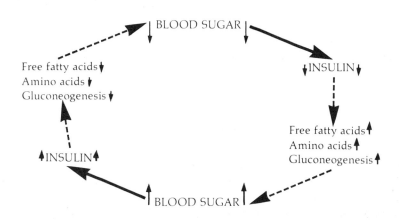

Figure 11. Regulation blood sugar level by insulin (via its effects on glucose production by the liver and mobilization of free fatty acids and amino acids).

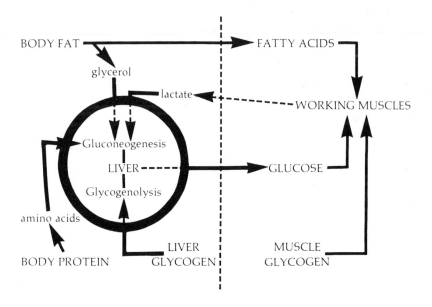

Figure 12. Derivation of fuel sources for working muscles

a replenishment of glycogen stores). The fasting state (and exercise) with low insulin levels, puts the transformer back into gear, breaking down its stores and increasing the uptake of raw materials to function as the glucose distributor for the body. With exercise, the output of glucose from the liver may increase by more than two or threefold. (In work of short duration, the increase is primarily an augmentation of glycogen breakdown, but there is a greater reliance on gluconeogenesis as exercise continues.)

Because of the fine regulation, and adaptations made to meet the increased energy demands, blood sugar levels change little during mild-to-moderate exercise, may increase somewhat with more severe exercise (attributed to the increased glucose production by the liver), and may decrease somewhat after extended exercise, though usually not to significantly low levels. Nonetheless, if liver glycogen stores are low (from prolonged exercise or low carbohydrate intake), and depleted fat stores restrict the availability of free fatty acids for energy needs, the liver may not be able to keep up with the glucose supplies demanded by exercise, and symptoms may result from significantly low blood-sugar levels (hypoglycemia).[31]

Now let's backtrack to the ballet dancer who feels lousy at four o'clock every day, and prefers to think that she suffers from a disease beyond her control (hypoglycemia) rather than to associate her fatigue with an overall poor nutritional status. Energy and vitality are commonly linked to blood-sugar levels, so lack of pep, fatigue, feeling down, or a poor performance is blamed on hypoglycemia, which apparently has become the trendy, catchall explanation for a hodgepodge of vague, nonspecific symptoms experienced while dancing or in daily life (a fact well recognized and exploited by certain food gurus and nutritional supplement promoters). Granted, various disease states do exist in which hypoglycemia may eventuate, accompanied by symptoms such as fatigue, spasms, sweating, palpitations, and numbness. But low levels of blood sugar may normally occur after meals—when metabolism shifts from the fed to the fasting state—without any symptoms.[32]

---

31.   Although genuine hypoglycemia with exercise is uncommon, it has been observed in marathon runners and in patients on low carbohydrate diets. I am aware of no studies of this type dealing exclusively with dancers, but it would seem likely that strenuous dancing, combined with a semistarvation carbohydrate regimen and low body-fat stores, could result in actual hypoglycemia.

32.   Park, B. N., Kahn, C. B., Gleason, R. E., & Soeldner, J. S. (1972), Insulin-glucose dynamics in nondiabetic reactive hypoglycemia and asymptomatic biochemical hypoglycemia in normals, prediabetics, and chemical diabetics, *Diabetes, 21,* 373.

An endocrinologist who deals extensively with dancers has frequently found "lowish" blood sugars in dancer patients, as well as other young, very thin women. Patients with complaints of "hypoglycemia" often report disappearance of the symptoms when placed on an adequate diet (and not necessarily a high-protein, low-carbohydrate "hypoglycemia" diet). This observation isn't in the least surprising. Quoting the physician:

> [The symptoms in these instances] are the result of terrible eating habits—call it whatever you want—but it's not a "disease" and I think it happens constantly among dancers. The main causes are just poor diet, stress, and the fact that these people are underweight. People have to eat well to feel normal, and women are more sensitive to their diets than men.

To adequately diagnose a hypoglycemic condition, a physician should demonstrate that symptoms occur simultaneously with a nadir in blood-glucose levels (some of the symptoms, such as sweating and palpitations, are the result of adaptive mechanisms, stress responses to low sugar levels intended to stimulate glucose output by the liver). The diagnosis, then, depends on two variables: the determination of an abnormally low blood-glucose level; and the association of symptoms with this level. Obviously, the first prerequisite requires some standard of what the normal range of blood sugar values is to begin with, and this is where the complexion of the medical profession was found to be blemished.

The normal range for fasting blood glucose is generally accepted to be within 60 and 100 milligrams glucose per 100 milliliters blood. It did not come to light until 1974, however, that the standard had been derived from control data from men and overweight women, but not from normal women. It was then demonstrated that, in normal women, blood-sugar levels do not necessarily stabilize at levels comparable to men;[33] in fact, they may occasionally dip to below 35 mg per 100 ml without any symptoms. Reasons postulated for this discrepancy include the smaller muscular compartment for women and the influence of female sex hormones in modulating tissue uptake and utilization of glucose. Regardless of the explanation, erroneous standards for hypoglycemia in the past have undoubtedly contributed to the overestimation of the prevalence of this condition by physicians, as well as to the rampant popular urge to claim oneself its victim. Articles in medical journal have since emphasized the

---

33. Merimee, T. J. & Tyson, J. E. (1974), Stabilization of plasma glucose during fasting: Normal variations in two separate studies, *New England Journal of Medicine, 291,* 1275–1277.

importance of distinguishing actual "chemical hypoglycemia" (which is treated by a low-carbohydrate, high-protein regimen and multiple meals) from the misattributed variety, termed "clinical pseudohypoglycemia" or "nonhypoglycemia."[34]

The main pitfall of any kind of misattribution is that the incorrect explanation may preclude the exploration of alternative explanations, and hence appropriate intervention and correction of the problem. In the more specific case of pseudohypoglycemia in the dancer, "treatment" may conceivably make matters worse. Consider the hypothetical case of the very thin dancer who pursues a rigorous work schedule despite sparse fat stores and a suboptimal intake of carbohydrate. She experiences lack of pep in the afternoon and concludes that she is a hypoglycemic (as we have seen, if her liver can't keep up with the glucose demands, a physiologic hypoglycemic state with symptoms might in fact arise). Mistaking pseudohypoglycemia for chemical hypoglycemia, she places herself on a high-protein, low-carbohydrate diet. Thus, a condition that may have been initiated by an insufficient amount of carbohydrate (and generally poor nutritional status) is "remedied" by cutting back on carbohydrates even further. With continuance or exacerbation of the symptoms, a nutritional vicious circle begins, making the dancer susceptible to further misattribution. ("If it isn't hypoglycemia, it must be Vitamin B deficiency, not enough Brewer's yeast," and so forth.)

34. See Meador, C. K. (1965), The art and science of nondisease, *New England Journal of Medicine, 272*, 92–95; Cahill, G. F., Jr. & Soeldner, J. S. (1974), A non-editorial on nonhypoglycemia, *New England Journal of Medicine, 291*, 905–906; Yager, J. & Young, R. T. (1974), Nonhypoglycemia is an epidemic condition, *New England Journal of Medicine, 291*, 907–908; Hofeldt, F. D., Adler, R. A., & Herman, R. H. (1975), Postprandial hypoglycemia: Fact or fiction?, *Journal of the American Medical Association, 233*, 1309.

3 The War with Water and Salt

Talk to a dancer about her weight, and you are apt to hear the phrase, "I retain water." Alas, a loaded statement. It seems almost a heartbreaking confession, a profound admission of a preordained curse or scandal.

"I am a deviant. Didn't you know? *I retain water.* No pity, please. Stoically shall I accept my fate, against all odds make special efforts and allowances to contend with my handicap. In the end, my talent shall reign supreme!"

Such a dramatic conception is not actually the case. Water retention is not a special disease, it is a normal phenomenon. In the words of a female endocrinologist:

> Every woman retains fluid. I retain fluid. I can wake up in the morning and I can have puffy eyes. But it doesn't matter to me. I'm not on stage and I'm not looking in a mirror all day long.

Cyclical variations in water weight, then, which many women experience and accept as a matter of course, often become an intolerable situation for dancers.

Five pounds of water may not be much for someone weighing 150 pounds, but for a 95 pound dancer, it's more than 5 percent of her total body weight. She can see it in the mirror and she can feel it. And then there are the constant reminders, such as having difficulty in hooking a costume or imagining a slightly louder grunt from a male partner performing a lift. But most important, the water weight unfortunately assumes the dimensions of a lost skirmish in the war against fat. In light of the innocently disguised but vindictive question, "Put on some weight?" fat and water become virtually indistinguishable, and the immediate response is the resolve to intensify dieting efforts. This works both ways, of course, for a compliment on looking "good" is a substantial morale booster, even if a diuretic is responsible. In either case, the actual amount of body fat may not have changed a fraction of an iota; only perceptions have altered, in what amounts to a self-involved game.

Although the difference in weight caused by water retention may be noticeable and distressing, the dancer's reaction to it is often completely out of proportion. An orthopedist related an example of this hypersensitivity, giving insight as well into some of the special difficulties a physician may encounter when dealing with dancers. In his practice, the orthopedist frequently prescribed the anti-inflammatory agent Butazolidin (phenylbutazone) for soft-tissue injuries. One of the side effects of this medication is retention of salt (and hence water), which completely resolves upon cessation of the drug but is nonetheless often unacceptable to the physician's dancer patients. At the mention of the drug:

> Right away they say "that puts on weight." Right away. They know it causes water retention, and they want to know if they can take a diuretic with it, or they won't take it unless you give them a diuretic with it. You have to explain to them that you're treating their present condition in time, and that as soon as the inflammatory stage is over, they discontinue the medication and the water will leave them.

It may, reports the physician, require considerable coaxing and compromising. Similarly, a number of dancers will not employ oral contraceptives precisely because of their water-retaining characteristics.

Water retention is a problem healthy men never have to deal with, since the fluid excess results primarily from the salt-retaining properties of the female hormone, "estrogen." During the premenstrual period (when estrogen levels are their highest), normal women show a slight gain of weight. The increase in weight during the premenstrual phase reaches a maximum value on the second day of menstruation, then follows a clear downward trend until the eighth day after menstrual onset.[1]

1. Robinson, M. F. & Watson P. E. (1965), Day-to-day variation in body weight of young women. *British Journal of Nutrition, 19,* 225–235.

In one study, an average weight gain of a pound-and-a-half occurred during the premenstrual phase in regularly menstruating women;[2] gains of three or more pounds in 30 percent of women during the premenstrual period have been reported.[3] The weight gain may occasionally be greater and may be accompanied by puffiness of the face and eyes and swelling of the feet or ankles. Toward the beginning of the period, or sometimes immediately after its cessation, increased urination causes rapid disappearance of the surplus reservoir. Of course, hormonal factors are only one variable in water balance, so let us step back for a broader overview in order to examine the dancer's dealings with matters liquid.

A Lesson in Water Balance

The ground rules for water balance are straightforward. The losses incurred through urine, feces, and sweat (as well by diffusion through the skin and the water vapor contained in exhaled air), must not exceed that which is supplied through intake of fluids, liquid content of foods, and the smaller quantity produced by the body during metabolism of food for energy. It is not possible for humans to adapt to or be physically trained to tolerate water intake lower than daily losses.

Under any circumstances, dehydration compromises the body's ability to function in a variety of ways—and dancing can only make matters worse. "Making weight" by combinations of food restriction along with fluid deprivation and dehydration are generally associated with a reduction in muscular strength, a decrease in work performance times, lower plasma and blood volumes, reduced heart functioning during submaximal work, a lower oxygen consumption, an impairment of thermoregulatory processes, a decrease in blood flow to the kidney and kidney filtering effectiveness, a depletion of liver glycogen stores, and electrolyte losses.[4]

To a great extent, a dancer's endurance is limited by the capacity of the circulatory system to provide oxygen and nutrients to the working

2.   As reported in Eston, R. G. (1984), The regular menstrual cycle and athletic performance, *Sports Medicine, 1*, 431–445.

3.   Reported in Novak, E. R., et al. (1970), *Textbook of gynecology*, (8th ed.), Baltimore: Williams & Wilkins.

4.   American College of Sports Medicine (1976), Position stand on weight loss in wrestlers, *Medicine and Science in Sports and Exercise, 8*, xi–xiii.

muscles. But the increased body heat produced by exercise also requires greater blood flow to the skin to dissipate heat by vaporizing sweat. Of course, there is a limited amount of blood for all these jobs (the blood volume of a 100 pound ballet dancer may be estimated at less than 3-1/2 quarts). The more sweating, the greater the amount of body fluids lost, and the less blood there is to go around. Spreading oneself (or one's fluids) too thin may impair performance and efficiency in early stages; carried to an extreme, it result in collapse (in some cases fatal).

The average adult water loss is in the neighborhood of 2 liters (slightly more than 2 quarts) per day; the daily average water allowance for adults is thus often quoted as 2.5 liters. For the individual of average activity, water intake and losses balance very closely, and daily weight fluctuations due to water are usually less than 1 percent of body weight. The athlete, on the other hand, may regularly incur a short-term negative water balance of 2 to 3 percent of body weight during daily exercise, and in some cases reach the critical 5 percent dehydration level. The capabilities for losses by sweating are awesome: an individual exercising vigorously in a hot environment can lose as much as 8 pounds of water in the form of sweat in an hour.[5]

Water intake must correspond to the increased water loss; free access to fluids is imperative to minimize dehydration and reduce the threat of overheating. Usually the sensation of thirst will govern replenishment over a twenty-four hour period (more than 5 pounds may be regained in a few hours after eating and drinking), although in some instances, with episodes of continued bouts of dehydration, thirst may be inadequate to insure sufficient intake. Caffeine-containing beverages, such as coffee, tea, and caffeinated sodas, should be avoided as means of fluid replenishment, since caffeine has a diuretic effect.

There are much more subtle mechanisms operating to maintain water and salt balance besides the sensations of thirst and hunger. For example, with training and heat acclimation, the concentration of a dancer's sweat becomes more diluted—an adaptation of the body to diminish salt loss. Although the sweat glands produce this modification, the principal responsibility for regulating water and salt balance is relegated to the kidneys. Both the amount of fluid excreted as urine and the salt concentration in the fluid are variable. In response to heavy sweating and periods of dehydration, the kidneys adjust accordingly, reducing the excretion of both salt and water.

5.   Williams, M. H. (1976), *Nutritional aspects of human physical and athletic performance*, Springfield, IL: Charles C. Thomas, p. 177.

Two hormones primarily mediate these modifications by the kidney. "Antidiuretic hormone" (ADH) is released by the pituitary gland under the control of a part of the brain called the hypothalamus. The mechanism is as follows: receptors in the hypothalamus detect changes in concentration of the blood; with water deprivation (or a relative loss of water from excessive sweating), more of the hormone is released into the blood stream, causing the kidney to excrete less water in the urine. The second hormone, "aldosterone," is secreted by the adrenal gland in greater amounts when the circulating blood volume is decreased (such as in a state of salt deficiency and dehydration). Aldosterone acts on the renal tubules, enhancing the body's reabsorption of sodium and chloride (potassium and hydrogen are lost in the process). The enhanced salt retention will secondarily lead to greater water retention.

Dancers and Dehydration

If one didn't know any better, one might get the impression that some dancers are intentionally bent on dehydrating themselves. The loss of body water is greatest in hot, humid conditions, because higher temperatures require more cooling and increased humidity decreases the ease with which the body moisture evaporates. If environmental conditions aren't bad enough, dancers often create their own personal hot house with rubber suits or layer upon layer of warm-up clothes. Worse yet, some will pursue sweat sessions while simultaneously restricting their intake of water and salt, an outlandishly stupid and dangerous practice.

A common notion is that one isn't working hard unless sweat is dripping. But since dripping sweat does not conduct the body's heat by vaporizing, it does not cool effectively. Hence, a puddle of water at one's feet represents a sacrifice of body fluids with very little cooling to show for it. Not that dripping sweat can be avoided; but if one sweats heavily, starting to drip might serve as a signal to remove a layer of warmings, or at the very least, to be sure to take an appropriate amount of water to compensate for increased losses.

"Diuretics" (water pills) enhance the excretion of body water, and hence may precipitate or compound dehydration. Nevertheless, individual athletes of all varieties—wrestlers, boxers, jockeys, lightweight crew—persist in employing dehydration techniques to make weight, and in my experience, dancers are no exception.[6] Diuretics are not indicated unless prescribed by a doctor, in which case they should be used gingerly (a hard-working dancer might be wise to be somewhat stoical about cyclical water retention). Physicians are sometimes inclined to dispense diuretics against their better judgment in an effort to appease stubborn and demanding patients. Also, a conniving patient may purposely exaggerate the extent of water retention in an effort to present a stronger argument for unnecessary medication.

Ironically, in their concerted efforts to rid themselves of water, dancers may actually be perpetrating the opposite condition—the subsequent (temporary) accumulation of even more water. This slap in the face by Mother Nature might occur under two similar conditions. I have already mentioned that the kidneys respond to a dehydrated state or salt deficit by increasing the production of the hormone aldosterone, thereby promoting sodium retention. Researchers have shown that when water is consumed freely during repeated workouts in the heat, the body actually retains salt (and thus water) to an increased extent.[7] In other words, repeated bouts of dehydration may eventuate in the body storing water in excess of the sweat loss. Thus, bundling up like an Eskimo and inducing dehydration may result in greater rehydration after one's thirst has been appeased (a phenomenon I call "Nanook's Revenge").

Similarly, it appears that people accustomed to low salt intakes may not excrete a heavy salt load effectively (possibly also owing to higher aldosterone levels). For instance, if a dancer who normally shuns sodium eats a salty pastrami sandwich for dinner, she may find herself more "blown up" than usual the next morning (an acute case of the "Post-Pastrami Puffs").

6.   The American College of Sports Medicine, in its Position stand, op. cit., recommends (among other things), that the "single or combined use of rubber suits, steam rooms, hot boxes, saunas, laxatives, and diuretics to 'make weight'" be prohibited.

7.   Smiles, K. A. & Robinson, S. (1971), Sodium ion conservation during acclimization of men to work in the heat, *Journal of Applied Physiology, 31*, 63–69; Costill, D. L., Coté, R., Miller, E., et al. (1975), Water and electrolyte replacement during repeated days of work in the heat, *Aviation, Space, and Environmental Medicine, 46*, 795–800.

Water and Dieting

For dieters, the contribution of water to the total amount of weight loss or gain can be frustrating and deceiving. Most of the total body weight is water, estimated as 60 percent in the average man and closer to 50 percent in the average woman. The difference reflects the fact that fatty tissue is only about 20 percent water, whereas muscle is nearly 75 percent; thus, the more muscular an individual, the greater the total percentage of body water. Women generally have more fat than men, but this may not be true in the lean, small-busted dancer with narrow hips, who in all likelihood contains even more water per pound than most males.

Knowing that such a high percentage of body weight is water, one may easily appreciate that rapid fluctuations in weight are always the result of fluid shifts and have nothing to do with the fate of fat. Any dieter tends to lose weight more quickly the first week or two of dieting, and much of this initial loss is water (in one study, 66 percent of the weight lost in the early phases of a diet was water).[8] Although the mechanism is incompletely understood, early or semi-starvation is characterized by increased sodium concentration in the urine and reduction in the concentrating ability of the kidneys, which would account for greater water losses. Additionally, as I have mentioned previously, protein and glycogen are incorporated into the body tissues along with water. Thus, as glycogen stores are depleted in fasting or carbohydrate deprivation, there is an obligatory water loss. Water losses are less of a factor in the later stages of a diet; in fact, water retention may even account for a gain in weight despite ongoing net losses of fat and protein.

The type of diet upon which one embarks also affects the amount of weight loss attributable to water. Since nitrogen, the byproduct of protein metabolism, requires water for excretion in the urine, excessively high protein intake can contribute to dehydration because of the need for the urinary excretion of excessive nitrogen.[9] A comparison of low-carbohydrate diets with mixed diets (both with the same numbers of calories) reveals that differences in weight loss are almost entirely attributable to the higher rate of water lost in the low-carbohydrate regimens.[10]

8.   Van Itallie, T. B. & Yang, M. (1977), Current concepts in nutrition: Diet and weight loss, *New England Journal of Medicine, 297,* 1158–1161.

9.   Steinbaugh, M. (1984), Nutritional needs of female athletes, *Clinics in Sports Medicine, (Symposium on Nutritional Aspects of Exercise), 3,* 649–670.

10.   Van Itallie, T. B. & Yang, M. (1977), Current concepts in nutrition, op. cit.

Self-imposed fluid restriction along with dieting compounds the problem—if food restriction is held constant when the volume of fluid being
consumed is decreased, more water will be lost from the tissues of the
body (relative to losses of fat and protein) than before the fluid restriction
occurred.[11]

Semi-starvation and severe carbohydrate restriction are also difficult
to sustain and not satisfactory approaches from the standpoint of meeting
a dancer's energy needs. As we have already seen, the most productive
loss of fat results from a steady restriction of caloric intake along with
increased energy expenditure over the long haul. In general, the quality
of weight loss is likely to be the highest (a high percentage of fat being
metabolized rather than increased losses of water and protein) when the
rate of loss is the slowest. Because the percentage of water loss is the
highest in the beginning stages of dieting, and the amount of water loss
can be accentuated and prolonged in dieters either on low-carbohydrate
diets or those simply fasting, we can understand one reason why so many
are thwarted in efforts to diet. In the beginning, when there is whole-
hearted conviction and dedication to the cause of dietary denial, the
weight loss shown on the scale is apt to be the greatest and psychologically most gratifying. As the resolve weakens with the passing days, so
does the positive feedback. A slip-up, such as succumbing to forbidden
or salty foods, causes increased fluid retention and thus discouragement
from the scale.

With so many factors coming into play—recurrent bouts of dehydration from sweating, normal physiological fluid shifts from hormonal
changes, unpredictability of eating behavior, and the variability with
which water is lost in various types (as well as phases) of dietary regimens—it is no wonder that one cannot always trust one's eyes when
looking a scale squarely in the face, or even when gazing at the mirrored
wall.

Electrolytes and Hypokalemia

Though salt loss always accompanies sweating, the concentration of
salt in sweat is only one-third to one-half that of the blood. Therefore,
relatively more water than salt is lost through perspiration, so the need

---

11. American College of Sports Medicine, Position Stand, op. cit.

for promptly replacing water is greater and more immediate than the demand for salt. Salt pills or special salt solutions are not necessary for consumption at the studio; a plain water fountain will suffice, provided the diet is adequate in replacing the salt losses at mealtimes. Sodium and chloride are the principal mineral elements in sweat; potassium and magnesium are lost in smaller amounts. Since these and other elements have the property of carrying an electrical charge when dissolved in solution (as "ions"), they are commonly referred to as "electrolytes."

Certainly, excessive sweating, in combination with poor or restricted dietary intake of salt and minerals, may result in a deficiency, such as low sodium levels ("hyponatremia"), hand-in-hand with dehydration. Despite the body's compensatory, salt-sparing mechanisms (such as decreased excretion of sodium in both sweat and urine during heat acclimation), dietary means dominate in the maintenance of water and electrolyte balance. Salt deficiency in a healthy individual can always be avoided by sensible eating and drinking; far from being an occupational hazard of the dance, it results from neglect. Sometimes more than neglect may be involved, however, which a consideration of potassium will reveal.

Potassium serves numerous important functions in the body: it is involved in energy-consuming reactions and the formation of high-energy compounds; it aids in the synthesis of glucose and glycogen; and its relative concentration (on the inside as compared to the outside of muscle cells) is instrumental in the normal functioning of muscles. The principal symptom of a deficiency of potassium ("hypokalemia") is marked fatigue, primarily due to the role of the ion in muscular contraction. A person may experience weakness or numbness, or in severe instances, partial or even complete paralysis (usually in the extremities). Other possible ramifications of hypokalemia include electrocardiographic changes, irregular heart rhythms (potentially fatal), and damage to the kidneys.

Because potassium is widely distributed in foods such as oranges, grapefruit, bananas, beef, and fish, and because the body is particularly efficient in controlling normal levels of this electrolyte, potassium deficiency is highly unlikely to develop under normal circumstances. The problem can nonetheless occur in dancers as the sequel of self-inflicted abnormal circumstances. Commonly, dancers who know something of hypokalemia—from first-hand knowledge or word of mouth—assume the condition to be the unavoidable result of heavy sweating. This is hardly the case.

As I have mentioned, a reasonable diet should be adequate to restore electrolytic balance in spite of excessive sweating. But in fact, potassium is not lost through perspiration to a large extent. The concentration of sodium in sweat is roughly ten times that of potassium; 9 pounds of sweat contain an estimated 6 to 8 percent of the body's sodium and chloride, but less than 1 percent of the body's potassium and magnesium.[12]

Then how can potassium deficiency come about? Aside from disease states (such as kidney disorders or diseases producing steroid hormones or requiring them for treatment), there are only two ways in which excessive potassium can be lost: (1) by rapid, heavy, or prolonged "diuresis" (urination); or (2) through the gastrointestinal tract (by vomiting or excessive diarrhea). Here is where electrolyte disturbances may be the direct consequence of self-abusive practices (Figure 13).[13]

The excessive diarrhea prompted by the habitual overuse of laxatives, as well as the increased urination induced by diuretics (especially the thiazide types, furosimide and ethacrynic acid), may substantially enhance potassium wastage. (Patients treated with potassium-losing diuretics for high blood pressure are either given potassium supplements or advised to ingest potassium-rich foods, and their potassium levels are intermittently monitored.) Continual and repeated vomiting results in a loss not only of ingested potassium-containing foods, but also the acid contents of the stomach (gastric juices). Prolonged, unreplaced loss of body acid (and accompanying chloride ions) may lead to the pH of the body becoming more alkaline, prompting the kidney to compensate by excreting more base (bicarbonate) in the urine. But along with the bicarbonate (and owing to the losses of chloride), the amount of potassium in the urine increases also. Thus, self-induced vomiting may account for greater potassium wastage through both the urinary and the gastrointestinal routes.

The specific problem of potassium deficiency is difficult to isolate from the general one of salt and water imbalance. For example, although perspiration may not be a major medium of potassium loss, loss of sodium may have an indirect effect. Recall that a state of low sodium with dehydration will induce greater retention of sodium by the kidney via the hormone aldosterone. The mechanism involves a trade-off of electrolytes; sodium is kept preferentially at the expense of a greater loss

---

12.   Costill, D. L. (1978), "The drinking runner," in Hal Higdon (ed.), *The complete diet guide for runners and other athletes*, Mountain View, CA.: World Publications, pp. 151–167.

13.   For examples of some of the ramifications of self-abusive practices, see deGraeff, J. & Schuurs. M. A. M. (1960), Severe potassium depletion caused by the abuse of laxatives: One patient followed for eight years, *Acta Medica Scandinavica, 166*, 407–422; Wolff, H. P., Vecsei, P., Krück, F., et al. (1968), Psychiatric disturbance leading to potassium depletion, sodium depletion, raised plasma-renin concentration, and secondary hyperaldosteronism, *Lancet, 1*, 258–261.

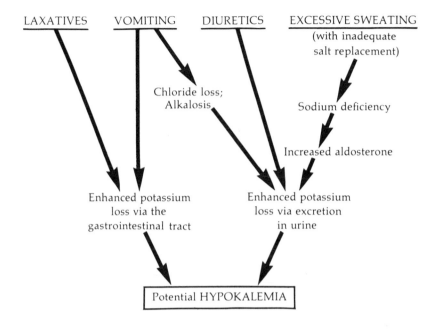

Figure 13. Mechanisms of increased potassium loss

of potassium in the urine. In this manner, excessive and unreplaced sodium losses may contribute to additional potassium wastage as the body attempts to remedy the deficit.

Since approximately 98 percent of the body's potassium resides within the cells, the amount in the blood—be it low, normal, or high—may not necessarily reflect the body's potassium status. The kidneys happen to be more responsive to high blood levels of potassium than to low ones, which is another manner in which subtle losses may occur. As potassium is closely related to stored glycogen, the breakdown of glycogen for energy may produce a temporary elevation of potassium levels in the blood, prompting the kidneys to excrete some of this excess in the urine. In this way, bringing the blood level back to normal contributes, in effect, to a gradual depletion of the total body stores, even though the blood level gives no indication of this. Potassium loss is a slow, insidious process.

A New York City physician described a teenage dancer patient who was so chronically deficient in potassium that she experienced paralysis in her feet and lower legs and compromised kidney function. Obviously this deficiency did not occur overnight, and the patient fervently denied any "wrong-doing" on her part. Patients often fail to admit to laxative or diuretic abuse, or to self-induced vomiting, which can greatly hamper a physician's clinical assessment. Certainly in matters such as these, experienced physicians have a high degree of suspicion. As one stated:

> I am convinced that many of the dancers [with electrolyte imbalances] who have told me things have just not told me the whole story. You may not always know what people do to themselves, because they lie to you constantly.

It is impossible to access the extent of hypokalemia in the dance world or to determine whether relative deficiencies might be related to some of the common complaints of dancers, such as weakness and fatigue. But in the healthy person subsisting on a reasonable diet, the condition should not occur. Nor, under normal circumstances, should potassium supplements be required for an individual (in fact, potassium supplements may be the cause of stomach upsets—besides, the liquid stuff tastes terrible). I am reminded of a dancer on voluntary water and salt restriction (and possibly laxative abuse), who sneakily attempted to second-guess physiology by self-prescribing over-the-counter potassium replacements. Although she avoided hypokalemia (her potassium levels were actually too high), she was foiled nonetheless, collapsing immediately after a performance because of dehydration and hyponatremia. At some point, foolishness will always tax the body beyond its gracious benevolence.

A Digression: On Leg Warmers

In the summer of 1924, a group of three singers, a conductor, and four dancers—under the name of the Soviet State Dancers—took leave from the Maryinsky Theatre for a summer vacation. State-sanctioned permission to cross the Baltic ultimately meant defection for the organizer of the tour, a baritone in the Maryinsky Opera Company named Vladimir Dimitriev, and the troupe of dancers, comprised of George Balanchine, Tamara Geva, Alexandra Danilova, and Nicholas Efimov.

After several lean and hungry years in revolutionary Russia, the troupe literally gorged on the abundant food available for the two-and-a-half days of the Baltic crossing, and at least as far as Alexandra Danilova was concerned, this was only the beginning. She described to me with relish the whipped cream and other culinary delights in which she indulged in Berlin, to the extent that in three months she had reached 130 pounds (a surplus of about 18 pounds).

At Danilova's first rehearsal with the Diaghilev company in Paris, the famous dancer Anton Dolin, faced with the prospect of having to partner such an abundant package, remarked to her: "You know what? I am not a piano mover, I am a dancer." It was the great impressario himself who presented Danilova with the ultimatum: either she would lose weight or Diaghilev would give her nothing to dance. At twenty, Danilova—who throughout her career at the Maryinsky had never been admonished about her weight—learned first-hand the metabolic facts of life of the dance world.[14]

Her reaction was to go immediately to a well-stocked pharmacy on the Champs Elysées, where she procured an unknown variety of diet pills (Madame Danilova only remembers that the packaging had "before" and "after" figures on it, one odiously fat and the other impressively thin). Convinced that the medication was the easy remedy to her problem, she raced back to her hotel with her purchase to initiate her diet. In her eagerness and desperation, Danilova fell victim to an all-too-common flaw in logic. The package directions called for one pill, one or two times a day. The ballerina said to herself, "One pill? Why one? I take five pills!"—a course of action which she followed, and which shortly thereafter resulted in her passing out.

Her next recollection was of Balanchine shaking her and inquiring about what had happened to his sick, trembling, and crying companion, and then condemning her for being so stupid as to resort to taking the pills. He offered instead some of his own dietary advice, which, as Danilova recalls, included eating meat and avoiding ice cream and other sweets. He also recommended that she take two daily lessons, and "get warm clothes." The purpose was to make her perspire, for as Danilova so wonderfully stated, with her Russian inflection, perspiration "to get all grease out" was of high priority in her weight-reducing regimen.

Danilova related how she cut the sleeves from an old sweater and used them as leggings. Nobody, according to Danilova, wore leg warmers in the Diaghilev Company at that time, but other members of the company

---

14.   Madame Danilova has related a portion of this story in her autobiography (1986), *Choura: The memoirs of Alexandra Danilova*, New York: Knopf, p. 73.

followed her lead, one by one. When the company went to London, the demand was such that Danilova ordered specially made pairs for herself and other dancers. The leggings, incidentally, were knit from oatmeal-colored yarn, more suitable than the shade of the originally sacrificed sweater (a detail which Madame Danilova couldn't recollect).

Thus the inauspicious, if not apocryphal, appearance of modern leg warmers on the dance scene.[15] It seems only fitting that their initial function was to warm the body specifically for the purpose of inducing weight loss through perspiration, rather than for other reasons. In fact, over the years the purpose of warmers has become increasingly obscure, which is quite in keeping with their debut.

One day, shortly before a dance class, I remarked offhandedly to an acquaintance that I was tired. It was a standard comment, meant to fill the sound void but not intended to be pursued further. I expected an equally perfunctory response, but the one I got was relatively thought provoking: "I bet you wouldn't be so tired and would feel better in class if you wore more clothes. You know, it makes you sweat and feel all greased up."

Now I wasn't exactly underdressed, being fully equipped with a dance belt, leotard, tights, and ballet slippers. Conspicuously absent, however, were warmers. It just so happened that on that day I had decided not to wear them (it was a rather warm studio, besides). Several thoughts struck me, but what really caught my ear was the word "grease," which Madame Danilova had used only the day before in a slightly different context. And in the various contexts of the word, I realized, rested the key to the true nature of leg warmers (a minor linguistic breakthrough).

In one sense, warmers cause you to "get the grease out," the old "weight loss is fat loss" misconception that has already been dealt with here. (I might add that if fat *were* lost by perspiring, fat droplets rolling off dancers in class would make dance surfaces hazardously slippery.) The other sense of the word "grease" is as a lubricant, something to oil and loosen up those rusting and creaking joints and tendons. This indirectly relates to the physiological benefits of heat, such as that produced by warming up. Muscle efficiency is enhanced at higher temperatures: in the neighborhood of 102–103° Fahrenheit, there is less resistance to

---

15. Mrs. Marian Ladre (formerly Illaria Obidenna), who attended the Petrograd school with both Balanchine and Danilova (and subsequently danced with the Diaghilev Company and the Ballet Russe de Monte Carlo), has informed me that "leggings" very similar to today's warmers were actually in use on Theatre Street, but only because the Russian studios had no heat.

stretch, and injuries are undoubtedly prevented by this muscular readiness.

Nonetheless, warmers are of limited and supplemental effectiveness even for warming. The best way to heat muscles is by working them. External methods of supplying heat—be they a heat pad, heating balms, or a hot shower—provide warmth to a very superficial depth. The deep muscles used in turn-out, for example, cannot be directly reached by these means (theraputically, physicians employ "diathermy," or deepheating methods). What warmers can do is insulate and retain some of the heat that results from muscular contraction. This is especially useful in cool studios, at the beginning of class when one's muscles are completely "cold," and in drafty backstage areas when there are periods of inactivity during a performance or rehearsal. As insulators, warmers are useful, provided they do not lead to overheating or dehydration. But they are never substitutes for a good preliminary warm-up or reasonable dieting.

There are two other functions of warmers, widely accepted though less publicized. Whether one envisions oneself as too thin or too heavy, bulky warmers make excellent camouflage. How can an instructor see enough flesh to make corrections when her pupil is bundled up to the extent that she resembles a cross between an Eskimo and the Michelin Tire Man? But the practice can be even more self-serving: it's the old "out of sight, out of mind" philosophy, supporting the specious syllogism: (1) I can't see my overabundant thighs; (2) you can't see them either; (3) therefore, they do not exist. Even a dieter who is chronically rubberized may admit, under extreme duress, that though she knows the weight loss is not fat but water, she persists in wearing the suit as a reducer simply because "it makes me feel better," which is certainly a valid reason.

Finally, warmers are a fact of life in the dance subculture. Regardless of the color or style (be they wool, acrylic, a blend, or rubber; storebought, homemade, or improvised), warmers are a part of the way dancers are supposed to look. One might even question if it is possible to call oneself a dancer in their absence. And the more layered, the more eclectic, the more haphazard-appearing, the better. Even a hot studio—with the sweat, the odor, the aching feet—can be a showcase for high fashion, what might be termed the "premeditated, reckless-abandon look."

Consider the girl who suggested I cover up to grease up. As I recall her in my mind's eye, she is fully clothed for the workout. The underlying tights and leotard are not visible. There is a full-length navy acrylic warm-up suit, a rubber suit with the pant legs rolled up to mid-thigh and held with a piece of elastic, an additional pair of aqua warmers, and gym socks over those. Just in case there should be a sudden chill from the north, she has an aubergine sweater draped around her shoulders and wears a headscarf. And if by some chance she should sweat, she has had the foresight to bring along a small hand towel which she has draped fastidiously over the *barre*. So burdened with clothes is she that she could probably do an entire variation inside of her self-styled shelter without there being the slightest indication of movement.

But what can I say? Admittedly, she is chic. And if one were to comment on her appearance, might she not say (like her equivalent arriving late at a party wearing a designer outfit): "Oh, these old things? I just got up this morning and threw on what happened to be there." Some people just know how to dress, I suppose (Figure 14).

So we owe a large debt indeed to Madame Danilova, who inadvertently inspired, for whatever reason, what has become a virtual necessity for dancers. Perhaps the import of that momentous invention can be rivaled only by the birth of the first dance bag. Is it even possible to imagine a world without dance bags, in which dancers transport their lambs wool and Bandaids in attaché cases?

Figure 14. What did this warmth-conscious as well as fashion-conscious dancer forget? A towel, draped fastidiously over the *barre,* just in case she should happen to perspire. (Photo by William H. Batson)

4 Foul Play with Food

The Laxative Purge

Historically, the use of cathartics or laxatives has been a mainstay of medical therapeutics (Figure 15). Purging (the elimination of waste from the colon), in fact, was one of the three basic treatments of ancient Greek medicine. The triad included bleeding (to get rid of the bad humours), starving (to prevent new ones from forming), and purging (to get rid of the rest, from whatever exit). This approach spread like wildfire over the Western world before it finally died out, and I mention it now only because some dancers still seem to adhere to the latter two-thirds of the triad.

But let's skip back over the scummy waters of history even farther for a moment to analyze the roots of this practice. The ancient Egyptians believed that internal decay was a cause of disease; the obvious solution, they reasoned, was to eliminate the source of possible decay in the

Figure 15. Purging with laxatives, one quick way to eliminate bad humours, as illustrated in this early-nineteenth-century plate by James Gillray, the foremost caricaturist of the period. (Courtesy of the Logan Clendening History of Medicine Library, the University of Kansas Medical Center)

intestines. Thus, the Egyptians became the all-time experts on enemas, and according to Herodotos:

> For three consecutive days in every month they purge themselves, pursuing after health by means of emetics and drenches; for they think it is from the food they eat that all sicknesses come to men.[1]

As only historical luck would have it, the Egyptian soil was—and still is—a generous source of *Ricinus communis,* the castor oil plant.

Traveling from the Nile to the Thames, we find that an empty stomach and scoured intestines were also prerequisites in the athletic training of oarsmen in nineteenth-century England. The use of enemas and cathartics for a body "purification" was considered indispensable in bringing the

1. Majno, G. (1975), *The healing hand*, Cambridge: Harvard University Press, p. 129.

organs of digestion to a healthy state of action. Getting into shape for those poor souls included vomiting and purging (antibilious pills, with salts, senna, and camomile), forced sweating (mandatory Turkish baths and long daily runs clad in heavy clothing), and a ludicrous diet (almost raw beef or mutton, stale bread, no vegetables, and a minimum of liquid). And how did this grisly discipline come to be regarded as the *sine qua non?* According to the medical commentator Sir Adolphe Abrahams:

> Because originally, feats and contests of pugilism, pedestrianism, or oarsmanship were confined to professionals, men of the lowest class whose lives were given to sloth, gluttony, intemperance, self-indulgences of every kind and the violation of all laws of hygiene, and in them a drastic curtailment of their customary habits was the most salutary precaution that could be framed and enforced.
>
> When sporting contests became fashionable, the gentleman-amateur passing from the rôle of patron to that of participant naturally adopted the methods of his professional *confrère*.[2]

We must not forget that the athletes of yesteryear were a far cry from their present-day counterparts, whose fame is such that their endorsement is sought for everything from deodorants to underwear. Even Galen, who took care of the Roman gladiators, held jocks in contempt. In his Exhortation of the Study of the Arts, he observed:

> When athletes miss their goal, they are disgraced; when they attain it, they are not yet even above brutes.[3]

Where the purification rite mutated into a dieting method is not clearcut. Of twenty-four ballet scholarship students in two company schools in New York City, one-third told me that they had used (or were using) laxatives for weight reduction or maintenance.[4] Almost a fad with the younger ballet dancers, laxatives appeared to be more commonly used

2. Abrahams, A. (1956), *The human machine.* Harmondsworth, Middlesex: Penguin Books, pp. 104–107.

3. From Ryan, A. J. & Allman, F. L. (eds.) (1974), *Sports medicine.* New York: Academic Press, p. 17.

4. In a recent survey of female collegiate athletes, 20 percent of the track and field competitors and 37 percent of the gymnasts reported having used laxatives for weight control. See Rosen, L. W., McKeag, D. B., Hough, D. O., & Curley, V. (1986), Pathogenic weight-control behavior in female athletes, *Physician and Sportsmedicine, 14,* 79–86.

in this age group than diuretics or self-induced vomiting; though for many who submit to self-abusive routines, the mode selected represents only a personal preference.

The inadvisability—not to mention the inconvenience—of cathartics may be overshadowed by the priority for maintaining a fat-free body. One fairly tall young dancer would only take laxatives the day before her adagio class, since she felt self-conscious and guilty for being so large, and wanted to give her male partners a break by weighing a bit less. Laxatives may be used to alleviate guilt or to atone for food indulgence or "binging"—as in the case of the young ballet corps member who steadfastly refuses to eat anything after seven in the evening, and relies on laxatives if she is unable to uphold her resolve.

The foolishness may be carried to the degree of mind-boggling stupidity. One teenage dancer was overdosing herself on four tablespoons of Epsom salts per day before she discovered that fluid retention was completely off-setting the "positive" benefit of "getting rid of the food I had the night before." Another aspiring ballet dancer described how she took laxatives off and on "when desperate," particularly while reducing from 120 to 110 pounds (her height was almost five-feet, four-inches). Her regimen had entailed one laxative (Ex-Lax) before meals, and two more pills after. She was taking as many as eighty pills per week when she finally stopped because of a friend's urging. It seems that the concerned friend (also a dancer) had an elderly aunt who had become "so messed up from laxatives that she had to wear a plastic bag." And as the reformed laxative abuser (who became a convert to diuretic abuse) reasoned, "You can't dance with something like that."

Even though the ancient Greeks did not have Ex-Lax, a wide variety of ingredients served them well (and not so well) as purgatives, such as large amounts of asses' milk and decoctions of melon, cabbage, and other plants, often mixed with honey. More drastic remedies were black hellebore, castor oil, and colocynth.[5] In general, cathartics act to increase the bulk and liquid contents of the feces by various mechanisms. Cascara and castor oil are irritants, producing rapid propulsion of the intestinal contents and thus preventing adequate time for the usual reabsorption of water. Inorganic salts (such as Epson salts) and indigestible fiber act as so-called "bulky" laxatives, increasing the volume of the contents of the gut (the salts do this by drawing in water and distending the intestine,

5. Castiglioni, A. (1941), *A history of medicine,* (Trans. E. B. Krumbhaar), New York: Knopf, p. 1754.

speeding up the transit time of the food). Mineral oil works essentially by lubricating, preventing some of the reabsorption of the fecal water contents as it passes through the bowel. Ex-Lax is a trade name of a laxative containing phenolphthalein, an agent widely found in proprietary nostrums. The precise mechanism of action of this cathartic remains to be determined (the cathartic effect of phenolphthalein was discovered in 1902 by a man named Vamossy, during a study undertaken for the Hungarian government to determine its safety as an additive for identification of artificial wines).[6]

Laxative abuse hampers the normal absorptive functions of the digestive system, increases the body's loss of potassium, and may lead to dehydration. Chronic overusers may ultimately develop "atonic constipation"—that is, a loss of adequate colonic muscular tone and a dependence on laxatives for excretory regulation. Cathartics have no place whatsoever in weight maintenance or reduction.

Self-Induced Vomiting

Vomunt ut edant, edunt ut vomant.
(They vomit to eat, and eat to vomit.)

Seneca, *Ad Marcian*

The Romans are given the dubious honor of having invented the vomitorium, where the overzealous feaster could empty his stomach after a heavy banquet. Some, as Seneca described, combining epicurianism with gluttony, would return to the table after vomiting to reappease their hunger. The custom is no longer with us, but the emphasis on slimness for the female in our culture rivals that demanded of women in epicurean Rome. Whether the practice was discreetly transmitted throughout the generations, or reinvented more recently, the vomitorium is still with us, though it may be only the toilet bowl in a campus sorority house.

When I first asked a group of ballet scholarship students (between the ages of 15 and 20) at a large New York City company school about

---

6.   Goodman, L. S. & Gilman, A. (eds.) (1975), *The pharmacological basis of therapeutics* (5th ed.), New York: Macmillan, p. 982.

vomiting as a means to maintain or lose weight, they cautiously exchanged looks until someone finally blurted, "You should have seen this place on Sunday nights [weigh-ins were on Monday]. Jeez." She started giggling, and the previously uncomfortable silence erupted into agreement and slightly embarrassed laughter. The secret was out, confession was good for the soul.

Inquiring further, I learned that "Nobody would eat anything past noon, and the whole second-floor bathroom [of the women's residence] would smell so bad that you couldn't use it." Some would even make last-minute preparations, vomiting up Monday morning's breakfast before heading to the studio.

Everyone in the group overwhelmingly claimed to know "others" who commonly vomited (as well as used laxatives and diuretics). They were obviously hesitant to admit to those transgressions themselves in a group setting, though a significant number of the young women present admitted to their participation on questionnaires and in individual interviews.

Aside from the natural repugnance that many people feel at the thought of forced vomiting, the possible deleterious effects outweigh even the aesthetic undesirability. Repeated vomiting (also called "emesis") may lead to dehydration, body mineral and pH disturbances from the loss of stomach acid secretions, swelling of the parotid glands, erosion of tooth enamel, esophagitis, and even rupture of the esophagus or stomach.[7] This isn't to say that a large percentage of vomiters inevitably will be stricken with such maladies; contributing factors include the frequency of vomiting, the amount and type of retained dietary intake, and the activity and constitution of the person involved. And fortunately, Mother Nature generously allows us considerable leeway in our dietary indiscretions (Figure 16), as the stubborn persistence of our all too human species readily attests.

What is more bothersome than the possible detrimental physical effects, though, is the attitude that these dancers must have or develop toward their bodies, as well as the extrinsic pressures that contribute to making vomiting a viable alternative. Whether done only intermittently or adopted as a routine, vomiting may be taught and reinforced by the dance milieu. An eighteen-year-old ballet company apprentice detailed her concerted efforts to make herself throw up (an act which disgusted her and which she had always had difficulty doing, even when sick as a

---

7. Herzon, F. S. & Kaufman, A. (1981), Vomiting and parotid enlargement, *Southern Medical Journal, 74,* 251; Herzog, D. B. & Copeland, P.M. (1985), Eating disorders, *New England Journal of Medicine, 313,* 295–303.

Figure 16. A nineteenth-century etching by H. Heath illustrates one of the many weight-reducing follies, the employment of a stomach pump.

A second caricature of the period depicts the action of emetics, an antiquated mainstay of medical therapeutics that has been perverted even further for svelte's sake. (Courtesy of the Logan Clendening History of Medicine Library, the University of Kansas Medical Center) child). She combined various ingredients that dancer friends had told her would induce vomiting (including milk, mustard, salt and pepper) only to find, to her dismay, that "it tasted good." Her experimentation with ipecac[8] was also unsuccessful (owing to her failure to drink ample amounts of water, necessary for the emetic to work). Thus repeatedly thwarted, this particular dancer decided that vomiting wasn't worth the the effort, so she contented herself with laxatives and diuretics.

A modern dancer in her mid-twenties who vomited three to four times per week recalled being "jealous as hell" over the vomiting of her best friend and roommate before embarking on the method herself, which she had now used for more than seven years. Nonvomiters may feel quite resentful of their vomiting peers, though they might never be prompted to indulge in emesis themselves. One ballet student expressed personal conflict and irritation over her roommate's habit, though it was never openly discussed and the latter dancer made token attempts to be clandestine by locking the bathroom door and running both faucets full force during the process. The nonvomiter was concerned for her friend's well-being but felt angry.

"She's cheating—it's not fair," she told me.

An interview with another young ballet student brought out the same conflict. Aware of the practice while at a performing arts school, she did not force vomiting herself until moving to New York, where she faced more rigorous competition and professional demands. To make matters worse, instructors and peers considered the thinnest girl in her ballet class "gorgeous," though the girl allegedly "vomited all the time, pigged-out constantly, and couldn't diet." At that point, the young dancer determined that there was "no reason I'm going to be heavier than everybody else."

During a six-month period, the seventeen-year-old vomited regularly at least three times a week, usually after the evening meal. She finally quit because of her growing disgust with the practice and with herself. Still, she was bitter at the injustice of it all—vomiting gave a competitive edge.

"It's cheating," she exclaimed, echoing her cohort's sentiments. "But they're just cheating themselves," she went on more quietly. The realization evidently not providing her much comfort, she became sullen.

8. Injudicious use of ipecac can cause a potentially fatal heart dysfunction. See Adler, A. G., Welinsky, P., Krall, R. A., & Cho, S. Y. (1980), Death resulting from ipecac syrup poisoning, *Journal of the American Medical Association, 243,* 1927–1928.

"But you have to compete with them," I said.

"I just want to be thin," she said flatly.

This statement came from a female measuring five feet, five inches in height, and in agony over her weight of 102 pounds.

"You're thin now," I said.

"I don't think so, I feel heavy. It feels so much better when I'm 95. That's how I was this summer [the time of her vomiting regimen]."

"I don't think it's unreasonable for you to maintain your weight at 102," I asserted.

"I look horrible at 102."

Again I had rammed into the brick wall of self-perception and arbitrariness of the concept of beauty. Logic and reason would be of no use in arguing a point of health. The subjective question of beauty is nowhere to be found in medical texts.

Self-induced vomiting isn't something people are willing to talk about, as many participants feel embarrassment, shame, or a "weakness of will." For others it may be a matter of course, a habit they are trapped in and almost compelled to maintain. In either event, the practice is usually well concealed. An administrator of a ballet company school (students from this school had first informed me of routine vomiting prior to weigh-ins), when asked if scholarship students vomited to keep their weight down, replied:

> Do I think it's done? I can't give you an answer because I don't live with these children and I am not aware of their habits when they leave here.

Another company school director told me:

> I suppose it goes on, but we have not heard anything in particular, not at all. But I know they diet; I know some of them have weight problems and have diet charts and that sort of thing.

Still another administrator in a ballet school was somewhat more informed, but reluctant to come out with it, understandably wishing to avoid the implication of school or personal responsibility. It was a simple yes-or-no question: "Do your kids vomit?" but the answer wasn't quite that simple:

"Well, the school was weighing them in every Saturday, and then we found out that they were doing some special, uh, things of not weighing that much on that particular day, like not eating the day before or I believe someone said something about laxatives or something or other like that."

"But were they throwing up?"

"Not that I know of. I don't know."

"So what did you do?"

"Obviously they were doing something wrong, so we switched the day, the time of weighing, when they wouldn't know when it would be; so they wouldn't do anything that would be harmful to themselves—unnaturally."

Now there's logic for you. Dance students do some things "unnaturally" in order to weigh less for a weigh-in; hence, if the exact time of the weigh-in is kept secret, then they won't know when to do their unnatural things, and the problem will be solved. That particular line of reasoning was one which I did not wish to pursue further.[9]

But let me not portray these teachers or administrators as ruthless Fagans, exploiting pathetic hordes of lost youths. Those who are aware of the situation (and truthfully, I believe that some are removed from the dancers to such an extent that they aren't) may be concerned and frustrated, and may even feel guilt about their implicit involvement. But the realities of the situation leave them impotent to effect change. There are practical concerns: the school must go on, talent must be developed, the vacated spots in the companies must be filled by the ranks of the lower echelons. The weak will fall by the wayside, trampled under the advancing armies in pink satin shoes and chiffon skirts.

We must be careful neither to exaggerate the prevalence of self-induced vomiting among dancers, nor to limit its presence to this population. Fourteen percent of 182 female collegiate athletes (many of them participating in sports in which extreme thinness is not at a premium) have reported having vomited as a means of weight control (within the group, nearly 30 percent of distance runners and over half of gymnasts have resorted to this practice on some occasion).[10] Self-induced vomiting exists throughout all strata of our society. Whether it be the "flipping" of jockeys or the dieting of models, actresses, or housewives, this practice pervades, and is bred by, a culture that equates thinness with beauty and success. I quote a female endocrinologist:

9.   Fortunately, weigh-ins are no longer generally employed, and many company schools (including the School of American Ballet) never demanded them of their dancers. Nowadays when a scale is brought out, it's most often used as a cudgel for the dancer who is too thin.

10.   Rosen, L. W. et al., Pathogenic weight-control behavior in female athletes, op. cit.

Take a female executive—your standard, terrific-looking, tough, put-together woman, and she goes to the bathroom and vomits after dinner . . . I don't think it happens to be normal to vomit after dinner. I'm not a big one for putting names on things—I just look and see if the behavior is healthy or not healthy for an individual. I think self-induced vomiting is not healthy.

With this statement I wholeheartedly concur. Self-induced vomiting is physiologically not á healthy practice. But there is a more important question that can't be answered as easily, Do psychologically "healthy" people vomit? Let us take a more personal glimpse of a vomiter who clearly suffers from an eating disorder that has a name—"bulimia"—before considering that question.

Portrait of a Bulimic

Miss X is in her late twenties and a modern dancer in a professional company. A dancer since childhood, she is a bright, articulate, college-educated woman, with a strong, well-proportioned, though slim, body of 110 pounds (and a height of approximately five-feet, four-inches). One would be hard-pressed to compare her to some of her frail young counterparts aspiring to be ballet dancers. She is older to begin with, and she is an established, seasoned performer. Although slender by most standards, she might be considered too heavy for classical ballet repertory in some companies, but for her type of dancing she requires the weight and the strength, and is aware that a weight loss of even 5 pounds is noticeably detrimental to her performing. She eats good food, has varied interests and talents, interacts well socially, and loves her work. She does not have any problems with cigarettes, alcohol, or drugs. Her problem is with food. Miss X is a bulimic, a food "binger" and chronic vomiter, who has been unable to get through a "clear" day (a day without vomiting at least once) in months.

Miss X describes herself as a "dieter" for as long as she can remember, consistently alternating between periods of overeating followed by semi-starvation, agonizingly denying herself food when she knew she had to lose weight for professional reasons (she has never, however, weighed more than 120 pounds). In her mid-twenties, she first learned a trick of the trade.

I had eaten too much for dinner . . . and I was going through agony because I still had been trying to lose weight . . . and I must have been so stupid because I could never figure out why those two girls [sitting across from her at the dinner table and partaking liberally from the salad bar] stayed so tiny and ate three times as much as I did. So they told me. At first it was difficult—you have those hang-ups that you have to be sick, it's distasteful—but it comes up the same way it goes down, it's so easy. When I got to the point where I discovered how easy it was—that everything I put down I could put right back up again—it took a tremendous pressure off. There was no denying anymore.

A regime of chronic vomiting involves a certain amount of logistics, and bingers devise their own methods and food preferences. Miss X described different "grades" of vomiters—those who can eat a mouthful of food and throw it up as opposed to those like herself who have to overeat considerably before emesis is possible. The vomiting can be induced by gagging oneself with a finger down the throat, or by developing simple muscular control. Miss X described her long torso, and noted that food sits high in her stomach after a binge; hence, she simply has to push on her abdomen to initiate the expulsion of its contents. A dancer friend of hers has always had a more difficult time of it, and sometimes resorts to placing something distasteful on her fingers to gag (usually a nail polish designed to discourage nail biting).

"Binge" foods are usually not exotic, and often will consist of whatever is around the apartment. A very practical consideration is expense. Miss X makes a point of rarely binging on junk food, since "sugar binging gives you the shakes . . . it's a tremendous shock to your system." A cardinal rule is to drink lots of liquids on a binge, especially milk, says Miss X. And there are certain foods that one avoids; for example, one intent on regurgitation would be ill-advised to eat a jar of peanut butter. I was informed that eating peanuts (with liquids) is preferable to eating peanut butter, but the latter can be managed in moderate amounts if it is consumed on warm toast. Following are excerpts from the interview, depicting her life-style and relationship with food:

Vincent: Did you throw up today?
Miss X: Yes.
Vincent: After breakfast?
Miss X: No, after lunch. I almost consistently make it through break-fast [which had consisted that morning of a part of a cantaloupe,

cottage cheese, coffee, and a variety of vitamins]. I usually binge at night after rehearsal.

Vincent: What did you have for lunch?

Miss X: Today I had a huge salad, then I had another salad, then I went out and got some chicken and some bread—I just ate about three good, normal meals—and then I had a box of Fig Newtons, over a quart of milk. . .

Vincent: Do you binge every day?

Miss X: I have been.

Vincent: What will you have for dinner?

Miss X: I don't know.

Vincent: Will you throw it up?

Miss X: I don't know: it's better not to plan those things.

Vincent: Do you eat when you're hungry?

Miss X: I have no idea anymore when I'm hungry and when I'm not.

Vincent: Do you enjoy eating?

Miss X: Yes.

Vincent: All that food?

Miss X: I enjoy it for awhile, then it gets uncomfortable and it isn't fun anymore. When you get to that point, the whole world stops—everything is totally tuned out. My whole focus is food, that's it.

Vincent: What's the most you've vomited in one day?

Miss X: Six times. That's just about eating from morning until night.

Vincent: Don't you get tired?

Miss X: You get exhausted, but it just doesn't stop.

Miss X has watched her gradual progression from a once-a-week vomiter to her present state: "In the beginning stages my excuses were 'I have to keep my weight down for dancing.' But it's like a child that's grown into a monster; it's so much more than that now. I just can't blame it on my dancing . . . it's far bigger than that."

She tries very hard not to vomit on performance days, because "if I do a lot of heavy binging or throwing up, and if I take laxatives, I know that I'm shaky, that I can hardly see straight." If she can get through three or four clear days, she feels stronger, but that isn't enough reinforcement to break the vomiting routine; she's tried many times to maintain a diet without binging, unsuccessfully. Her addiction has reached the point where she has made excuses while on a date so that she could go home and continue binging by herself.

Binging is by nature isolating—it takes time and is not feasible socially or in public places. But the binger is mentally as well as physically isolated. Few, if any, people may know the secret—not the family, not the choreographer, perhaps not even the spouse. In fact, one of Miss X's greatest fears is for someone to walk in on her during a binge. People are naturally shocked, and justifiably ill-equipped to deal with a problem that can often be quite a clinical challenge to a psychiatrist. For this reason, Miss X has been reluctant to reveal her practice even in close relationships with men. Only recently has she become open about her binging with close friends who are not bingers themselves.

Miss X knows other dancers who are bingers and describes them as all different, with different reasons for their eating disorder. She views her own problem as a disease of a hundred faces:

> One day it's because it's frustration, another day it's something else. And I'm wondering what it will take to stop; whether I'll be frightened to death at some point, because I ultimately know it's very harmful. I don't think that the average person has to go out on a stage and be bigger than they are, and that's part of what's demanded of me. I'm constantly trying to transcend either my own emotions or my physicality; then I have to go home at night, and face my physicality, my emotions—a lot of things I just can't handle. It's my way of tuning out, of not thinking, of blotting out absolutely everything.

And so she struggles with the frustration and the guilt ("five binges later, and you turn around and look at yourself, and it's really awful"). She doesn't want her binging to run her life; she sees the waste of energy involved in "putting two hours into something financially draining, mentally draining, physically draining." And yet, much as she would like to solve her problem,

> The very fact of having to go back—which is the worst agony? Having to go back and be on a very restricted diet; I'm not looking to get rid of this problem and have another one to replace it.

Miss X says of herself: "I'm a good dancer, I'm strong, I'm reasonably healthy"—which makes her feel all the more terrible when young, admiring dance students ask her how she manages to keep so thin. "'Well, look at me—I eat thirty Hershey bars and ten dinners every night. That's how I keep so thin.' Is that what I'm supposed to say? So I don't answer them. I change the subject. I would never do that to somebody else."

The Defense

Miss X is a striking and extreme example, and by using her as an illustration I in no way wish to suggest that vomiting is necessarily addictive. In our consideration of normal versus abnormal behavior, we might place her at one end of the following hypothetical continuum:

1. Anne came home for the holidays, and finding her mother's cooking so much better than college dormitory food, she ate too much at the family dinner. She went for a walk but with no relief. Finally, as a result of her stomach discomfort, she made herself vomit, something she had never done before.
2. Sue is dieting, and she learned from a friend that she can vomit after a large meal if she loses her will power and breaks her diet. She has felt guilty enough to do this about five or six times this year.
3. Gloria has always been a poor dieter, but has found that an effective way to lose weight is to vomit whenever she goes off her diet, which is often.
4. Miss X is a compulsive eater, binging on large amounts of food and vomiting afterwards. She doesn't know why she eats, but is unable to control her behavior, which at this point is detrimentally affecting her everyday life and relationships.

Since eating behavior depends on a variety of internal and external factors, at what point does one draw the line? Anne's behavior appears fairly understandable, but it becomes a question of degree. Anne overate one time and vomited and Sue does it rarely; but then we get to Gloria and finally to Miss X, whose vomiting is extensive and even perceived by herself as a major problem. The issue is complex, but we are being inaccurate in identifying the vomiting as the central issue. Whether or not vomiting is ever appropriate, it is a response or a defense—perhaps a defense against heaviness, or against uncontrollable eating, or against failure in a job or competition. Vomiting isn't a disease, it's a symptom, and may equally result from intestinal flu as from a distortion of body image.

Whatever the circumstances, in time a symptom such as vomiting may come to take on a life of its own. In a sense, all psychiatric symptoms are very much like an addiction, in that a whole new set of dynamics is set in motion by the presence of the symptom, and that the symptom itself may be sustained by factors quite independent of those which precipitated it to begin with. With vomiting, there may be a habituating effect. For example, a vomiter may feel constantly hungry and dehydrated, and because of that, will eat or drink more, thus bringing on the feeling of fullness, the guilt, and therefore the need to vomit again.

"Bulimia" (which literally means ox hunger) is a fairly general term referring to a broad range of binge eating behavior. "Bulimia nervosa," a more precise psychiatric term reflecting an extreme preoccupation with body image, can be diagnosed in a standardized manner by a physician according to criteria from the third revised edition of the American Psychiatric Association's *Diagnostic and Statistical Manual* (DSM III-R) (See Table 1).[11] The reported prevalence of bulimia in the general population varies widely;[12] in one survey of American college students, 19 percent of the female population experienced major symptoms of bulimia, and purging behavior (laxative use and/or self-induced vomiting) occurred in an average of 10 percent of students of both sexes.[13] In another more recent study of 1,728 tenth-grade students, purging behavior (vomiting, use of laxatives or diuretics) was reported in 13 percent, females outnumbering males two-to-one.[14]

I must again stress here that vomiting by itself is not necessarily an expression of deep-seated psychological problems or even indicative of the presence of a clinical eating disorder. A recent study compared a group of seventy-seven college and ballet students who engaged in vomiting with a group of women who never vomited and also with a group of bulimia nervosa patients. The vomiting group of students was shown to be a highly varied population, only 10 percent of whom scored at or above the level of bulimia nervosa patients on a psychological test designed to identify eating disorders (this test, the *Eating Disorder Inven-*

---

11.   For those wishing to delve further into bulimia and eating disorders in general, there is certainly no shortage of reference materials. In fact, *The International Journal of Eating Disorders* is a medical journal devoted exclusively to research into these types of problems. For a starter for the general reader, I recommend Boskind-White, M. & White, W. C. (1983), *Bulimarexia: The binge/purge cycle.* New York: Norton.

12.   This variation relates to differences in sampling techniques (surveys often have a small percentage of respondents and hence an increased likelihood of bias); the potential inaccuracy of self-reporting (especially since the definition and meaning of the term "binge eating" can be ambiguous); and the limitations of psychological testing when used in isolation (without personal interviews).

13.   Halmi, K. A., Falk, J. R., & Schwartz, E. (1981), Binge-eating and vomiting: A survey of a college population, *Psychological Medicine, 11,* 697–706.

14.   Killen, J. D., Taylor, C. B., Telch, M. J., et al. (1986), Self-induced vomiting and laxative and diuretic use among teenagers. Precursers of the binge-purge syndrome?, *Journal of the American Medical Association, 255,* 1447–1449.

Table 1. DSM-IIIR Diagnostic Criteria for Bulimia Nervosa (1987)

A. Recurrent episodes of binge eating (rapid consumption of a large amount of food in a discrete period of time).
B. A feeling of lack of control over eating behavior during the eating binges.
C. The person regularly engages in either self-induced vomiting, use of laxatives or diuretics, strict dieting or fasting, or vigorous exercise in order to prevent weight gain.
D. A minimum average of two binge eating episodes a week for at least three months.
E. Persistent overconcern with body shape and weight.

Reprinted with permission from the *Diagnostic and Statistical Manual of Mental Disorders, Third Edition, Revised.* Copyright © 1987, American Psychiatric Association, pp. 68–69.

tory, or *EDI,* will be discussed in more detail in the next chapter). The authors concluded that "relying upon self-induced vomiting or simple measures of weight preoccupation without considering other dimensions of psychological functioning is of limited value in identifying the presence of a clinically significant eating disorder."[15]

Margaret Mead insisted on the need to take into account the sociocultural framework of food habits, and this is easy to appreciate in the case of a model, a jockey, and a dancer. To a lesser extent, it applies to all of us, from the businessman who wants the physique of a professional athlete to the secretary who wants to look like a cover girl, all in the interest of greater happiness and success. A fifteen-year-old girl seeking a dance career may be entering a world in which the image conceived for woman is a distortion of usual standards. If she lives in a dormitory where a significant number of her friends vomit before a weigh-in, one might not label her participation in that practice as "abnormal behavior." It is therefore much easier for me to conclude that the environment is unhealthy than to comment on the psyche of an adolescent girl.

Weight loss and maintenance within appropriate physiological boundaries is always possible by reasonable and conventional methods. However, if expectations are unrealistic, neither these nor hazardous and unconventional means will ultimately be of any use. I do not know of any dancers who, having attained their desired weight by vomiting, have then ceased the battle. They constantly struggle, reinforcing their own unhealthy patterns and behavior, victimized by their obsession. Whether vomiting represents normal or abnormal behavior is subjective and perhaps academic; that it is unhealthy is difficult to dispute.

15. Olmsted, M. P. & Garner, D. M. (1986), The significance of self-induced vomiting as a weight control method among nonclinical samples, *International Journal of Eating Disorders, 5,* 683–700.

5 Anorexia Nervosa and the Dancer: The Slender Balance

In the month of July she fell into a total suppression of her Monthly Courses from a multitude of Cares and Passions of her Mind . . . From which time her Appetite began to abate, and her Digestion to be bad; her flesh also began to be flaccid and loose, and her looks pale . . . I do not remember that I did ever in all my practice see one, that was conversant with the Living so much wasted with the greatest degree of Consumption (like a skeleton only clad with skin) yet there was no Fever, but on the contrary a coldness of her whole body.

Description of Mr. Duke's daughter in St. Mary Axe, who became ill in July, 1684, in her eighteenth year, from *Phthisiologia: or, a Treatise of Consumptions*, by Richard Morton, 1689

In a board game called The Ballet Company, the object is to attain the status of *prima ballerina assoluta* by moving a playing piece around a board blanketed with a variety of professional obstacles (Figure 17). If one happens to roll a six on the first toss of the dice, landing on a square

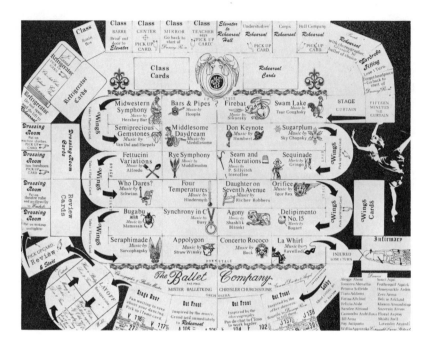

Figure 17. Reproduction of the game board of The Ballet Company Game, which contained (in a Refrigerator Card) the first published reference to anorexia nervosa in the context of the ballet world. (Courtesy of Stetson Enterprises)

which orders the procurement of a Refrigerator Card, one might pick up a card saying: "Avoid eating for two entire weeks. Company sends you to a psychiatrist who diagnoses anorexia nervosa. Lose 1 fame card."[1]

Thus, as Richard Morton is commonly credited with the first description of anorexia nervosa (1689) in the medical literature (Figure 18), to my knowledge the first published reference to anorexia nervosa in the context of dance is on the aforementioned Refrigerator Card, published in 1973. That some dancers carry their weight obsession "a little too far" is well recognized in dance circles; and although most teachers and choreographers feel that the majority of weight problems are on the heavy end of the spectrum, the "too thin" dancer is highly visible.

The questions then arise: Is anorexia nervosa—a syndrome characterized by self-induced starvation leading to profound weight loss—more prevalent in the dance world than in the general population? And if so,

---

1. *The Ballet Company: A Game for Dancers and Balletomanes of All Ages.* Copyright © 1973 by Lynne Stetson.

Figure 18. Frontispiece of *Phthisiologia: Or, a Treatise of Consumptions,* in which Richard Morton is credited with the first description of anorexia nervosa in the medical literature. The affliction of Mr. Duke's eighteen-year-old daughter was termed a nervous atrophy, or *Atrophia vel Phthisis nervosa.* (Courtesy of the Logan Clendening History of Medicine Library, the University of Kansas Medical Center)

what is the nature of the relationship between the dance experience and this entity? Certainly anorexia nervosa has received much attention in both the lay press and the medical literature, and some studies indicate that its incidence has increased dramatically over the past two decades (although greater recognition of the entity, and perhaps even "overdiagnosis" may be partially responsible for its seeming upsurge). In any event, let us briefly overview anorexia nervosa in fairly general terms, and then consider it from a dance perspective.

The "Relentless Pursuit of Thinness"

The young woman at Over-Haden . . . began (as her mother says)
to lose her appetite in December last, and had lost it quite in March
following: insomuch as that for the last six months she has not eaten
or drunk anything at all, but only wets her lips with a feather dipt
in water.

Thomas Hobbes, in a letter from
Chatsworth, October 20, 1668

Miss K. R., age fourteen, had been a plump, healthy girl until the
beginning of 1887, at which point she began, "without apparent cause,
to evince a repugnance to food; and soon afterwards declined to take any
whatever, except half a cup of tea or coffee." By the time she visited the
house of Sir William Gull (Figure 19), physician to Guy's Hospital in
London, on April 20, she was extremely emaciated, so much so as to be
the object of remark to passersby as she walked through the streets. At a
height of five feet, four inches, she weighed only 63 pounds. Her extremities were blue and cold, her pulse somewhat slow (46), and her
temperature slightly below the normal standard (97°). Nonetheless,
physical examination showed no sign of organic disease, and the patient
"expressed herself as quite well."[2] (Figure 20).

The case of Miss K. R., which appeared in the March 17, 1888 issue
of the *Lancet,* was the last contribution to the study of clinical medicine
by Sir William.[3] The case report of anorexia nervosa was an appropriate
coda for the physician who had coined the term fourteen years earlier in
the *Transactions of the Clinical Society,* stressing the loss of appetite
(anorexia) rather than the pronounced loss of flesh. Sir William believed
the want of appetite to be due to a "morbid mental state," since the fact

---

2.   Gull, W. W. (17 March 1888), Anorexia nervosa, *Lancet, i,* pp. 516–517.

3.   William Withey Gull (1816–1890), who served as Physician in Ordinary to Queen Victoria, is
quite an intriguing historical figure. In Steven Knight's (1977) book *Jack the ripper: The final*
solution (London: Grafton), Knight claims that Sir William "invented" the heinous Jack and played
an instrumental role in the brutal Whitechapel murders. Ostensibly, Victoria's grandson, Prince
Albert Victor ("Eddy"), had secretly wed a Catholic commoner and fathered a daughter by her. Gull,
an influential member of the government's inner circle, allegedly arranged the kidnap of Eddy's wife
and committed her to a lunatic asylum. Subsequently, the East End prostitutes who knew of the
affair were systematically silenced.

Figure 19. An "Ape" (Carlo Pellegrini) caricature of William W. Gull, which appeared in the December 18, 1875 issue of *Vanity Fair*. (From the author's collection)

"that mental states may destroy appetite is notorious, and it will be admitted that young women at the ages named are especially obnoxious to mental perversity."[4] Incidentally, the two case histories presented in 1874, as well as that of Miss K. R., culminated in recovery, though mention was made of a case with a fatal termination.

Since its classical description by Gull, anorexia nervosa has remained an enigma to medicine, as reflected by the voluminous literature concerning this "rare" syndrome. The confusion of our predecessors as well as the difficulties encountered by current investigators in part stem from the complex and dynamic nature of the disorder. Symptoms referable to the psychological components of the problem are intermingled with those

4.   Gull, W. W. (1874), *Transactions of the Clinical Society of London, 7*, 22. Sir William, in a medical address at Oxford in the fall of 1868, mentioned a "peculiar form of disease" which he termed "apepsia hysterica." In a paper in the *Archives générales de Médecine* of April 1873, a Dr. Lasègue described the malady as "hysterical anorexia." By 1874 Sir William, evidently, without being aware of the publication of the French journal, had decided himself that "anorexia" was a more appropriate term than "apepsia." Thus, anorexia nervosa became a clinical entity almost simultaneously with the independent reports from England and France over a century ago.

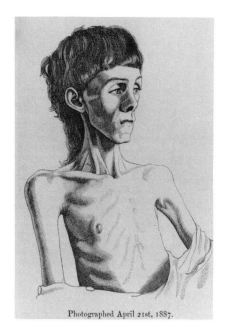 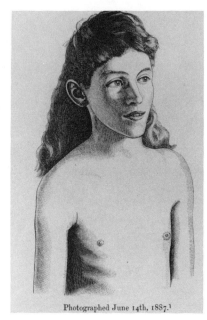

Photographed April 21st, 1887.   Photographed June 14th, 1887.[1]

Figure 20. Before-and-after engravings of Miss K. R., first seen by Sir William Gull in April 1887 and reported as a case history of anorexia nervosa in the *Lancet*, March 17, 1888.

that result from nutritional deprivation. Excessively rigid control over eating may ultimately result in a symptom complex which is essentially one of starvation: "amenorrhea" (cessation of menstruation), severe constipation, "hypotension" (low blood pressure), "hypothermia" (low body temperature), "bradycardia" (slow heart rate), and hormonal changes which include a low thyroid hormone, low "gonadotropins" (hormones stimulating sexual glands), and elevated steroids (more specifically, corticoids).[5]

Along with the psychological factors that might serve to instigate the eating behavior are the influences upon thinking, feeling, and behavior which result from the self-induced malnutrition. Cause and effect become muddled and indistinguishable:

5.   Of the numerous review articles, I would recommend the following: Warren, M. P. & Van de Wiele, R. L. (1973), Clinical and metabolic features of anorexia nervosa, *American Journal of Obstetrics and Gynecology, 117,* 435–449; Warren, M. P. (1985), Anorexia nervosa and related eating disorders, *Clinics in Obstetrics and Gynecology 28,* 588–597; Herzog, D. B. & Copeland, P. M. (1985), Eating disorders, *New England Journal of Medicine, 313,* 295–303.

When you lose that much weight—and especially after vomiting—
you can't make sense out of things. I found that I couldn't do really
simple things. I'd go to the store and forget what I went for. That
happens once in a while to people, but to me it would happen all the
time. I felt like I was in a constant state of confusion a lot of times.
I got lost on the subways; I'd get on and then forget where I was
going, or forget to get off and not know where I was, and be too
weak to walk up the stairs and get out of the subway.[6]

It is erroneous to equate anorexia nervosa with simply "going overboard" on a diet. The late Dr. Hilde Bruch, one of the foremost experts
an anorexia nervosa and other eating disorders, referred to the "relentless
pursuit of thinness."[7] More striking than the emaciation is the irrational
denial—denial of hunger, denial of being "too thin." It is both frustrating
and horrifying to watch a young woman almost hellbent on starving
herself to death, yet refusing to admit to any problem:

In a weird sort of way you find that you take pride in the way you
look; even though you know you're getting thinner, you feel real
good about it because it's one thing not too many people can do.
Even though you may realize other things may be happening that
aren't good from your weight loss, you still feel like you're rising
above everybody else.

Denial of hunger implies that the term "anorexia nervosa" is actually
a misnomer; rather than a true anorexia, or loss of appetite, the anorexic
is preoccupied and constantly obsessed with food. Anorexics are often
excellent cooks, forcing their creations on others but refusing to partake
themselves. An all-consuming preoccupation with food, typified by such
eccentric manifestations as food hoarding, ritualistic eating habits, and
excessive binging and purging, is termed "anorectic behavior," and appears similar to behavior patterns common to all starvation victims:

6.   The unidentified quotations in this section are taken from personal interviews with five women
who sustained severe weight losses and generally conformed to the accepted criteria for anorexia
nervosa. Two of the five required hospitalization at some point, and all either are, were, or aspired
to be professional ballet dancers.

7.   See the following excellent treatments of the entity: Bruch,H. (1973), *Eating Disorders: Obesity, anorexia nervosa, and the person within.* New York: Basic Books; Bruch, H. (1978), *The
golden cage: The enigma of anorexia nervosa,* Cambridge: Harvard University Press.

When you get that far into the whole thing, you feel guilty about almost anything you put into your mouth. If I would eat a potato chip or something, I would go to the bathroom and make myself vomit. Or if I'd eat a couple of carrot sticks. I'd really want the food so bad—I was so hungry—but I felt like I just couldn't let myself have it. I'd also chew food up and spit it out, so people around me would think I was eating. You learn a lot of little tricks like that, like hiding food under things on your plate, like lettuce.

Another aspect of behavior that is seen in many anorexics is hyperactivity, which seems even more pronounced in light of the emaciation. Sir William Gull had remarked on this aspect in his case descriptions of 1874; Miss A (5'5", 82 pounds) "was restless and active. This was, in fact, a striking expression of the nervous state, for it seemed hardly possible that a body so wasted could undergo the exercise which seemed agreeable." Concerning the second case, Miss B, he observed: "Notwithstanding the great emaciation and apparent weakness, there was a peculiar restlessness, difficult I was informed, to control. The mother added 'She is never tired.'"

I took two modern classes in the morning—which are pretty strenuous—and then would walk across Central Park over to the West Side to take a two-hour ballet class, and then walk back home again. Sometimes I'd stop on the way home to swim laps—I'd get in and swim lap after lap after lap after lap; my muscles would start cramping, and I literally could not stand up when I got out of the pool. I was blacking out from not having the energy to go on.

The following quotation conveys a sense not only of the extent of hyperactivity, distortion, and obsession concerning the body, but also of the difficulties that may be encountered early in treatment:

When I went into the hospital [for anorexia nervosa] my weight went even lower. They were trying to put me on a special kind of diet, and I would throw away a lot of the food, order salads instead of what they put on the menu. . . . I also decided that I couldn't get enough exercise in the hospital, so I'd close my door and do a special exercise class on the floor . . . and then I'd sneak out of my room and run up and down the stairs—about twelve flights of stairs—as many times as I could. I mean, I don't remember what was the most times—probably twenty times—but it would take me a good forty-five minutes to an hour to do the stairs. That's running, up and down, as fast as I could; the whole time marking up at the top on the fire extinguisher box how many times I had been up there. [Unable to keep track of the number of times, she had made hash marks on the dusty box with her finger and saliva.]

For those who have had little exposure to the problem, the presence of an anorexic can be quite disconcerting. The situation is even more difficult for family and close friends, since pleading and reasoning are of no avail to one who can't "see" realistically, who, regardless of the degree of thinness, is looking into a "fat" mirror. Because of this, anorexics become isolated and self-absorbed, avoided by acquaintances who feel strained and uncomfortable around them, and often alienated from and antagonized by well-intentioned loved ones:

I was really lonely. Because if you're around people, you have to eat . . . so I would make up excuses to have to go home, or have a shower, or have to do something, to avoid mealtime. And people don't really enjoy being around you that much either. I know I got on people's nerves just to be around; and they'd be embarrassed about wanting to eat because I wouldn't be hungry or wouldn't eat, or even worse, I would convince everybody to break their diets and go for ice cream, and then I would just take a bite. I wouldn't blame them if they hated me.

The rigid control over eating and excessive concern with the body are not themselves the problem; rather, they are symptoms of underlying factors. According to Dr. Bruch, the "relentless pursuit of thinness" is in itself a late symptom reflecting three pre-illness features of altered psychological functioning: (1) severe disturbances in body image; (2) disturbance in the accuracy of perceiving or recognizing body states, such as failing to recognize nutritional needs; and (3) an underlying sense of ineffectiveness, a conviction of helplessness in changing one's life.[8]

I think the whole problem comes down to feeling that forces outside of you are making you do this; that you aren't doing it to yourself. You feel like other people are making you do things all the time; you feel out of control with everything in your life, except your body. And this rigid sort of dieting/exercise thing is ultimate proof

---

8. Bruch, H. (1966), Anorexia nervosa and its differential diagnosis, *Journal of Nervous and Mental Disease, 141,* 555–566.

of your strict control over yourself, control over your eating and not eating.

Patterns and Parallels

To know what kind of person has a disease is as essential as to know what kind of disease a person has.

Francis Scott Smyth

Statistically, anorexia nervosa is most prevalent among adolescent girls from "stable" middle and upper-class families (it is extremely uncommon among males and blacks). The parents are usually self-assured, the mother often a woman of achievement (or career woman frustrated in her aspirations), the father typically successful, preoccupied with outer appearances, and admiring fitness, beauty, and achievement. The families are seemingly well-functioning, but tend to gloss over or deny conflict and have difficulty adapting to stressful circumstances. The children themselves are characteristically overachievers and "strivers," "never-any-trouble" children who are judgmental and who demand that others live up to the rigid value system by which they function. They may be socially isolated and overly concerned with being found wanting or not living up to expectations. Often the onset of weight loss is associated with the confronting of new experiences, in which the adolescent is faced with some changes or demands with which she is ill prepared to cope.[9]

Comparing the prototype for anorexia nervosa with the aspiring dancer in classical ballet suggests a number of parallels. To begin with, both populations consist primarily of adolescent girls. As a New York psychiatrist noted:

---

9.   In presenting this simplified portrait, I have drawn primarily from the works of Dr. Bruch and from Minuchin, S., Rosman, B. L., & Baker, L. (1978), *Psychosomatic families: Anorexia nervosa in context*, Cambridge: Harvard University Press. Additionally, for a comprehensive treatment on a variety of aspects of anorexia nervosa, see: Vigersky, R. A. (ed.) (1977), *Anorexia nervosa*, monograph of the National Institute of Child Health and Human Development, New York: Raven Press; Brownell, K. D. & Foreyt, J. P. (eds.) (1986), *Handbook of eating disorders: Physiology, psychology, and treatment of obesity, anorexia, and bulimia*, New York: Basic Books.

> Many of these girls [ballet students] are getting into or going through puberty; their bodies are changing at precisely the time when demands are being made on them to really control their bodies; when there's a known upsurge in eating desire—adolescents eat more—and where problems in self-esteem and self-confidence are characteristic of the developmental age. So you've got a lot of influences all operating at the same time.

Not unusually, a young girl encouraged to study dance comes from a middle or upper-class home, where high value is placed in achievement and on artistic pursuits, and where money is available to finance them. Once the student decides to pursue a dance career seriously, the encouragement and sacrifices required of the family may be considerable. This family support, along with the parental statement "I want you to have all the opportunities I never had," may also entail considerable expectations—the frustrated mother who "lives through her children," offering sacrifices with strings attached. In this way, the "anorexic mother" may be sadly reminiscent of the stereotypical stage mom, putting additional demands on her progeny, imparting to them a concern about not living up to expectations, a fear of being a disappointment to their parents. A dance teacher and choreographer observes:

> A lot of these kids are not dancing really because they want to dance, they're dancing because they're being pushed by mothers. Which is fine—I mean, sometimes you need to be pushed—but a lot of times it's so artificial. And then if the child doesn't get a scholarship, then she's no good, and they go through the whole thing that they won't let the kid dance if they have to pay for it and then the kid feels that she's failed.

As has been abundantly illustrated, the dance world is characterized not only by exhausting physical exercise, but also by the necessity for control, by the striving for artistic and technical proficiency, and by the overwhelming emphasis placed on the fashionable "look" and the consequent preoccupation with the body. The young dancer coming to New York to pursue a career in dance will face other changes and demands that are also challenging and stressful, pressures that have nothing to do with competition and the need for attainment of a level of professional competency. A company ballet school administrator is sympathetic:

> When we speak of the young dancers coming to New York for the first time, living in residences, living in apartments, having to

struggle financially, this becomes a tremendous burden, many taking jobs after classes. It's so hard, it's so sad.

Another such administrator gives an idea of what's expected:

> The fourteen-year-olds have academic school at 8:30, one or two subjects; they run home for [dance] class until 12:00. At 12:00 they run back to Professional Children's School where they eat something in the cafeteria, then they have academic subjects again until 2:00. At 2:00 they run like crazy, come back here, and have a [dance] class. And after that they may or may not have another [dance] class at 5:30 to 7:00, and they still have their homework to do.

In pointing out the potential similarities between the prototypical "anorexic" environment and the dance environment, I am not insinuating that the dance directly causes anorexia nervosa. As we shall see, however, there is ample evidence that cultural factors are related to the pathogenesis of this disorder (the earliest evidence, in fact, came from studies of ballet dancers). The possibilities are twofold. I quote a New York City psychiatrist who has worked extensively with this disorder:

> I would think that in the kind of person vulnerable or predisposed to anorexia, dancing is the kind of experience that is likely to bring out that vulnerability or predisposition. [A dancer is] so into [her] body, so attuned and sensitive to her body, that somebody whose own body image is precarious to begin with is obviously going to be much more vulnerable to the situation than somebody who has gone into a more cerebral field.

And concerning the second possible relationship:

> Certainly, one would expect that people with some of the characteristics of anorexia might go into dancing. By that, I mean, we know anorexics tend to be hyperactive; we also know that they are very much into their bodies; we also know that they're strivers, people who want to accomplish things. And fourth, these are not only people who are strivers, but they are people who have some talent. Given a fifth ingredient; namely, some early exposure to the dance, or family influence in the dance, it's not surprising that they may move in the direction of the dance.

The empirical observation that anorexia nervosa is over-represented in the dance population was first shown statistically by two Canadian researchers, Drs. David M. Garner and Paul E. Garfinkel, leading researchers in this field for the past decade. The *Eating Attitudes Test* (EAT), an objective questionnaire useful in detecting anorexia nervosa, was administered to a group of dance students, patients of comparable age with anorexia nervosa, and a control population of university students. The results, shown in Table 2, revealed that the mean score on the test of the dancers was intermediate between the control and anorexic group, with anorexia diagnosed among 5 percent of their dancers. They concluded that:

> these data support the hypothesis that individuals who focus increased emphasis on body size are at risk of anorexia nervosa and related dieting problems and that cultural variables may play a significant role in interacting with psychobiological forces in the development of anorexia nervosa in vulnerable adolescents. These findings are also compatible with the possibility that anorexic individuals may selectively enter dance schools or that high performance expectations per se rather than augmented focus on body size may facilitate the development of the syndrome.[10]

This report appeared as a letter to the editor of the *Lancet* on September 23, 1978, 104 years after Sir William Gull's classical description of anorexia nervosa in the same medical journal.

Table 2.   EAT Scores and Prevalence of Anorexia Nervosa

Group	No.	Mean age (S.D.)	Mean E.A.T. Score	Score symptomatic of anorexia*	Primary anorexia nervosa
Anorexia nervosa	33	22.5 (7.0)	58.9	33 (100%)	33
Controls	59	21.8 (2.8)	15.6	4 (7%)	0
Dance	112	20.2 (3.3)	25.5	31 (28%)	6

*As defined by a score of 32 or greater on the eating attitudes test.
The Lancet, Vol. 2, 1978, p. 674. Reproduced by permission.

10.   Garner, D. M. & Garfinkel, P. E. (1978), Sociocultural factors in anorexia nervosa (Letter to the Editor), *Lancet, 2,* 674.

An expanded version of Garner and Garfinkel's report was first presented at the American Psychological Association Annual Meeting in Toronto in 1978, and subsequently at the American Psychiatric Association Meeting in Chicago in 1979. The expanded study included 183 professional dance students at three national calibre professional dance schools in Canada, all evaluated with the EAT, and compared with female university students, music students, modelling students, and anorexia nervosa patients.[11] Sixty-nine dancers (38 percent) displayed EAT scores above the normal cut-off (≥ 30), compared with 9 percent of the university and music students. Twelve cases (6.5 percent) of anorexia nervosa were diagnosed in the dance group. Excessive dieting concerns and anorexia nervosa were also over-represented in the modelling students. When the dance students from the more competitive schools were analyzed as a group (one of the three schools had more academic and less professional focus), 45 percent of the students scored above the cut-off, and anorexia nervosa was diagnosed in 8 percent.[12] These findings were shocking, particularly since the highest incidence for anorexia nervosa previously reported for an independent or boarding-school setting was 1 percent.[13]

At the Chicago meeting, Dr. Eugene Lowenkopf and I presented a related paper, a report on the eating behavior of 55 serious young dancers in New York City. In 8 of these young girls, weight loss at some point became significant enough to warrant concern from peers, instructors, or the dancers themselves, although only one dancer had been hospitalized for this condition.[14] In that report, we were "forced to conclude that there is an anorexic syndrome endemic to young female ballet dancers, the psychological roots of which we could not ascertain."

As a given, the etiology of anorexia nervosa remained unclear. But what made everyone concerned more uncomfortable was that the factors

11.   Garner, D. M. & Garfinkel, P. E. (1980), Socio-cultural factors in the development of anorexia nervosa, *Psychological Medicine, 10,* 647–656.

12.   In a recent study of university dancers (students enrolled in intermediate and advanced dance technique classes), 33 percent scored above the normal cut-off on the EAT, compared with 13.8 percent of nondancing undergraduates. See Evers, C. L. (1987), Dietary intake and symptoms of anorexia nervosa in female university dancers, *Journal of the American Dietetic Association, 87,* 66–68.

13.   Crisp, A. H., Palmer, R. L., & Kalucy, R. S. (1976), How common is anorexia nervosa? A prevalence study, *British Journal of Psychiatry, 218,* 549–554.

14.   Lowenkopf, E. L. & Vincent, L. M. (1982), The student ballet dancer and anorexia, *The Hillside Journal of Clinical Psychiatry, 4,* 53–64.

differentiating the severe, "clear-cut" case of anorexia nervosa from the milder presentation of anorexic symptoms were similarly unclear. Did anorexia nervosa represent a distinct diagnostic entity, or simply an extreme point on a continuum of concern about weight? Where was one to place the much larger group of dancers who behaved in many, but not all ways, like anorexia nervosa patients? For instance, how did one classify the eighteen-year-old ballet student who is obsessed with her look, who may abuse laxatives or induce vomiting, and considers herself obese at any weight over 95 pounds?

In these pages I have referred to a number of young dancers who manifest these characteristics, who are very thin by almost any standards (except their own), and who even drop to lower body weights. Often the weight loss is initiated as a consequence of an increased dancing schedule (such as a move to New York City), a career opportunity (a crash diet of Tab and bubble gum three days prior to an audition), poor eating habits (lousy residence-hall food without kitchen facilities and not enough money to eat out), or downright unrealistic demands of others. A ballet scholarship student described how these demands could lead to unhealthy weight loss:

> A couple of summers ago I probably had a mild case of anorexia nervosa. I had a bowl of bran in the morning, and that was it for the whole day, for a whole summer. Because my director sort of brainwashed me that I was obese (I was like I am now—five feet, two inches, 95 pounds) and he wanted me to look like a toothpick. He sort of brainwashed me so I didn't know how far I was going. I got to about 80 pounds.

Nonetheless, an important distinction differentiates most dancers, such as the one quoted above, from the classical anorexic: the presence of a safety valve, the absence of the irrational denial. Perhaps, one could argue, it is a matter of the degree to which they "see" unrealistically. At some point they may become frightened, no longer like the way they look, notice a loss of strength that is detrimental to their dancing, or decide that dancing just isn't worth it.

There's a basic confounding problem here; namely, the definition of our terms (and, perhaps more important, the continued use of an antiquated one). Labeling can clarify, but it can also confine and limit, resulting in even more ambiguity. And the more confused physicians are, the more labels they bestow. (One could make the argument that the amount of understanding is inversely proportional to the number of names applied.) Consider a sampling of some of the terms that have sprouted around "anorexia nervosa" and other eating disorders:[15] "true anorexia nervosa," "mild anorexia nervosa," "atypical anorexia nervosa," "subclinical anorexia nervosa," "pseudo-anorexia nervosa," "anorexic-like," "anorectic behavior," "anorexoid," "bulimia," "bulimia nervosa," "bulimarexia," "dietary chaos syndrome," "gorging disorder," "evacuation abuse disorder," "partial syndrome," "pursuit of thinness disorder," "weight-preoccupied," "thin-fat."[16] One New York City psychiatrist who has worked with dancers, feeling uncomfortable with any direct reference to anorexia nervosa, speaks simply of "neurotic excesses." Another physician balletomane has referred to "gentle starvation," which I find particularly annoying and deserving of a place right besides "a little pregnant." Personally, I wouldn't mind a bit if "anorexia nervosa" were relegated back to the nineteenth century, where it originated and where it may still belong.

Unfortunately, for the time being we appear to be stuck with "anorexia nervosa" and all the semantic havoc it has produced. And if terminology and classification is a problem for the medical community, it's much more of a problem for the rest of us out there. For example, in a recent survey, 22 percent of Caucasian American ballet dancers in national companies reported that they have "had" anorexia nervosa![17] This is incredibly far-fetched, and illustrates the ignorance and confusion that currently exists. Obviously, self-diagnosis bears little relationship to the actual prevalence of the disorder or disorders.

So what's in a name, anyhow? Let's continue by reviewing the basis for the diagnosis of anorexia nervosa, because a disease can't be diagnosed until it has been defined. Or can it?

15. See the following: Button, E. J. & Whitehouse, A. (1981), Subclinical anorexia nervosa, *Psychological Medicine. 11*, 509–516; Russell, G. (1979), Bulimia nervosa: An ominous variant of anorexia nervosa, *Psychological Medicine, 9*, 429–488; Boskind-White, M. & White, W. C., Jr. (1983), *Bulimarexia: The binge/purge cycle*, New York: W. W. Norton; Lowenkopf, E. L. (1982), Anorexia nervosa: Some nosological considerations, *Comprehensive Psychiatry, 23*, 233–240; Garner, D. M., Olmsted, M. P., Polivy, J., & Garfinkel, P. E. (1984), Comparison between weight-preoccupied women and anorexia nervosa, *Psychosomatic Medicine, 46*, 255–266.

16. "Thin-fat people," a term coined by Dr. Hilde Bruch, refers to those persons who succeed in keeping their weight close to or below normal, but whose lives are centered upon the maintenance of this low weight, and who tend to interpret a slight gain as gross fatness.

17. Hamilton, L. H., Brooks-Gunn, J., & Warren, M. P. (1985), Sociocultural influences on eating disorders in professional female ballet dancers, *International Journal of Eating Disorders, 4*, 465–477.

Drawing the Line

Physicians think they do a lot for a patient when they give his disease a name.

Immanuel Kant

We don't have a high percentage of that [anorexia nervosa] around here; we have people who are naturally thin—very thin. And some of them I really stay on their tail to keep enough food in their bodies while they're working; you know, not to be too tired and forget to eat.

Company ballet school instructor

As previously shown, medical terminology carries an implicit authoritativeness, whether the terms are accurate or not. While many illnesses are understood (in the sense that their causes have been precisely determined), others are not. And when the etiology of an illness is not known, a collection of characteristic symptoms is often used to make a diagnosis and gather a population for study. Even when we don't know exactly what we're dealing with, we can always describe what we see. A collection of symptoms establishes a "syndrome." Anorexia nervosa, from its inception, has been diagnosed in precisely such a manner.

When a seeming increase in anorexia nervosa was observed in ballet dancers in the latter part of the 70s, the diagnosis was based upon criteria, published in 1972, of Dr. John Feighner and associates (see Table 3).[18] Subsequently, the criteria most often employed for the diagnosis of anorexia nervosa became those established by the American Psychiatric Association first in 1980 (DSM-III) and subsequently revised in 1987 (DSM-IIIR) (see Table 4).[19] All of these criteria groupings represent an aggregate of characteristics constituting the typical picture of anorexia nervosa, established on the basis of empirical and statistical evidence.

---

18.   Feighner, J., Robins, E., & Guze, S. B. (1972), Diagnostic criteria for use in psychiatric research, *Archives of General Psychiatry, 26*, 57–63.

19.   American Psychiatric Association (1980), *DSM III: Diagnostic and statistical manual of mental disorders* (3rd ed.); American Psychiatric Association (1987), *DSM IIIR: Diagnostic and statistical manual of mental disorders* (3rd rev. ed.).

Table 3.   Feighner Criteria for the Diagnosis of Anorexia Nervosa. For a diagnosis of anorexia nervosa, A through E are required.

A.   Age of onset prior to 25.
B.   Anorexia with accompanying weight loss of at least 25% of original body weight.
C.   A distorted, implacable attitude towards eating, food, or weight that overrides hunger, admonitions, reassurance and threats; e.g. (1) Denial of illness with a failure to recognize nutritional needs, (2) apparent enjoyment in losing weight with overt manifestation that food refusal is a pleasurable indulgence, (3) a desired body image of extreme thinness with overt evidence that it is rewarding to the patient to achieve and maintain this state, and (4) unusual hoarding or handling of food.
D.   No known medical illness that could account for the anorexia and weight loss.
E.   No other known psychiatric disorder with particular reference to primary affective disorders, schizophrenia, obsessive-compulsive and phobic neurosis. (The assumption is made that even though it may appear phobic or obsessional, food refusal alone is not sufficient to qualify for obsessive-compulsive or phobic disease.)
F.   At least two of the following manifestations. (1) Amenorrhea. (2) Lanugo. (3) Bradycardia (persistent resting pulse of 60 or less). (4) Periods of overactivity. (5) Episodes of bulimia. (6) Vomiting (may be self-induced).

From *Archives of General Psychiatry* (1972), *26*, 57. Copyright © 1972, American Medical Association.

These criteria are by no means absolute; in part they are subjective and even when they appear objective they are in part arbitrary (particularly arbitrary are defining cut-offs, such as the percentage of weight loss needed to qualify).

We recognize immediately that criteria based upon the general population are clearly slanted against dancers, that these criteria do not make allowances for a very special subculture with values and patterns of behavior at variance with the larger culture. Without question, many young ballet students in New York City and elsewhere: (1) attain or maintain a weight significantly below a "standard" based on the average woman, not the average dancer; (2) evidence a pattern of behavior aimed at inducing weight loss; i.e., constant dieting; (3) admit an aversion to regaining a "normal" weight, a normal weight not being appropriate dancing weight; and (4) do not have menstrual periods (as we shall learn in detail in the next chapter).

Classification especially presents a problem in the dance world, where defining a "case" of anorexia nervosa may prove quite difficult, given that key features of the disorder may be either very common or not able to be quite appropriately applied. One child psychiatrist has stated that "several sessions with the dieting dancer may be necessary to arrive at

Table 4.   DSM-III Diagnostic Criteria for Anorexia Nervosa (1980)

A. Intense fear of becoming obese, which does not diminish as weight loss progresses.
B. Disturbance of body image, e.g., claiming to "feel fat" even when emaciated.
C. Weight loss of at least 25% of original body weight or, if under eighteen years of age, weight loss from original body weight plus projected weight gain expected from growth charts may be combined to make the 25%.
D. Refusal to maintain body weight over a minimal normal weight for age and height.
E. No known physical illness that would account for the weight loss.

Reprinted with permission from the *Diagnostic and Statistical Manual of Mental Disorders, Third Edition.* Copyright © 1980, American Psychiatric Association, page 69.

DSM-IIIR Diagnostic Criteria for Anorexia Nervosa (1987)

A. Refusal to maintain body weight over a minimal normal weight for age and height, e.g., weight loss leading to maintenance of body weight 15% below that expected; or failure to make expected weight gain during period of growth, leading to body weight 15% below that expected.
B. Intense fear of gaining weight or becoming fat, even though underweight.
C. Disturbance in the way in which one's body weight, size or shape is experienced, e.g., the person claims to "feel fat" even when emaciated, believes that one area of the body is "too fat" even when obviously underweight.
D. In females, absence of at least three consecutive menstrual cycles when otherwise expected to occur (primary or secondary amenorrhea). (A woman is considered to have amenorrhea if her periods occur only following hormone, e.g., estrogen, administration.)

Reprinted with permission from the *Diagnostic and Statistical Manual of Mental Disorders, Third Edition, Revised.* Copyright © 1987, American Psychiatric Association, page 67.

an accurate diagnosis."[20] And from their experience with dance students in England, Szmukler and coworkers stated that the "high level of background 'noise' [here referring to the ubiquitous weight and menstrual disturbances and weight preoccupation] tended to obscure the 'signals' which would usually be of diagnostic significance."[21]

In an attempt to measure the symptoms of anorexia nervosa and provide a screening method for detecting previously undiagnosed cases in high-risk populations, psychological testing has been widely and increas-

20. Maloney, M. J. (1983), Anorexia nervosa and bulimia in dancers: Accurate diagnosis and treatment planning, *Clinics in Sports Medicine, 2,* 549–555.

21. Szmukler, G. I., Eisler, I., Gillies, C., & Hayward, M. E. (1985), The implications of anorexia nervosa in a ballet school, *Journal of Psychiatric Research, 19,* 177–181. Among one hundred students of a British ballet academy, in which the "matron reacted strongly to girls with a marked drop in weight and insisted that it be regained promptly," seven "possible" students with anorexia nervosa, when followed up after one year, had continued to dance and were considerably improved in their physical status without medical intervention.

ingly utilized. I have already referred to the Eating Attitudes Test (EAT),[22] which is reprinted in its entirety in Table 5 with the kind permission of Dr. Garner. The EAT is comprised of three distinct clusters of questions which relate to: (1) dieting—items intended to reflect an avoidance of fattening foods and a preoccupation with being thinner; (2) bulimia and food preoccupation—items reflecting thoughts about food as well as those indicating bulimia; and (3) oral control—items relating to self-control of eating and the perceived pressures from others to gain weight. It is crucial to note that most "high scorers" do not, in fact, satisfy the diagnostic criteria for anorexia nervosa. A major limitation of the EAT is that, while it may indicate the presence of disturbed eating patterns, it does not reveal the motivation or potential psychological disturbances causing the behavior.

This inherent shortcoming has been overcome in the Eating Disorder Inventory (EDI), more recently developed by Dr. Garner and coworkers (Table 6). This 64-item test is comprised of eight separate sections or subscales. Three of the subscales reflect attitudes and behavior ("Drive for Thinness," "Bulimia," and "Body Dissatisfaction"); the remainder evaluate specific psychological traits that are associated with anorexia nervosa ("Ineffectiveness," "Perfectionism," "Interpersonal Distrust," "Interoceptive Awareness," and "Maturity Fears"). The EDI is designed to identify and differentiate subgroups of individuals with eating disorders, and distinguish those with serious psychopathology from "normal" dieters. As we shall see below, the use of this test is now only beginning to clear up the murky waters.

Refining and Redefining

Anorexia nervosa is an illness; ballerinas are not sick.

R. G. Druss and J. A. Silverman

I have pointed out the common traits between anorexics and certain ballet dancers; what needs to be stressed again are their differences. This is not to deny that there are dancers who indeed suffer from anorexia

---

22.   Garner, D. M. & Garfinkel, P. E. (1979), The Eating Attitudes Test: An index of the symptoms of anorexia nervosa, *Psychological Medicine, 9,* 273–279. The original version of this test, containing 40 items, was subsequently abbreviated to 26 items. See Garner, D. M., Olmsted, M. P., Bohr, Y., & Garfinkel, P. E. (1982), The Eating Attitudes Test: Psychometric features and clinical correlates, *Psychological Medicine, 12,* 871–878.

Table 5.   Eating Attitudes Test (EAT-26) items*

1. Am terrified about being overweight.
2. Avoid eating when I am hungry.
3. Find myself preoccupied with food.
4. Have gone on eating binges where I feel that I may not not be able to stop.
5. Cut my food into small pieces.
6. Aware of the calorie content of foods that I eat.
7. Particularly avoid foods with a high carbohydrate content. (e.g. bread, rice, pota-toes, etc.).
8. Feel that others would prefer if I ate more.
9. Vomit after I have eaten.
10. Feel extremely guilty after eating.
11. Am preoccupied with a desire to be thinner.
12. Think about burning up calories when I exercise.
13. Other people think that I am too thin.
14. Am preoccupied with the thought of having fat on my body.
15. Take longer than others to eat my meals.
16. Avoid foods with sugar in them.
17. Eat diet foods.
18. Feel that food controls my life.
19. Display self-control around food.
20. Feel that others pressure me to eat.
21. Give too much time and thought to food.
22. Feel uncomfortable after eating sweets.
23. Engage in dieting behavior.
24. Like my stomach to be empty.
25. Enjoy trying new rich foods.
26. Have the impulse to vomit after meals.

*Scored according to responses of "always," "usually," "often," "sometimes," "rarely," or "never"

Reprinted courtesy of Dr. David Garner

nervosa (or anorexics who happen to dance), or that the incidence of true anorexia and other significant eating disorders is substantially higher in the dance world and in other occupational settings. And while the symptoms of anorexia nervosa may be adaptive in dance, they nonetheless have serious negative health consequences.[23]

23. Garner, D. M., Garfinkel, P. E., Rockert, W., & Olmsted, M. P. (1987), A prospective study of eating disturbances in the ballet, *Psychotherapy and Psychosomatics, 48,* 171–176. The suggestion of Szmukler et. al. (in Implications of anorexia nervosa, op. cit.) that less significance should be attributed to these symptoms because they are common and because ballet students "improve in their physical status without medical intervention" is disputed. Followup studies on ballet students showed that while most of the students with anorexia nervosa had gained weight, many of these individuals continued to experience disturbed attitudes toward food and their bodies.

Table 6. Eating Disorder Inventory (EDI) subscales and sample items

Drive for Thinness
  "I am preoccupied with the desire to be thinner."
  "I am terrified of gaining weight."

Bulimia
  "I stuff myself with food."
  "I have gone on eating binges where I have felt that I could not stop."

Body Dissatisfaction
  "I think that my stomach is too big."
  "I think that my thighs are too large."

Ineffectiveness
  "I feel ineffective as a person."
  "I have a low opinion of myself."

Perfectionism
  "I hate being less than best at things."
  "I have extremely high goals."

Interpersonal Distrust
  "I am open about my feelings." [negatively keyed item]
  "I have close relationships." [negatively keyed item]

Interoceptive Awareness
  "I get confused about what emotion I am feeling."
  "I have feelings I can't quite identify."

Maturity Fears
  "I wish that I could be younger."
  "I wish that I could return to the security of childhood."

Adapted and reproduced by special permission of the Publisher, Psychological Assessment Resources, Inc., 16102 North Florida Avenue, Lutz, Florida 33549, from The Eating Disorder Inventory by D. Garner, M. P. Olmstead, & J. Polivy, Copyright © 1984. Further reproduction is prohibited without permission from PAR, Inc.

In one of the more interesting psychological assessments of serious young ballet dancers, Dr. Richard Druss (a psychiatrist) and Dr. Joseph Silverman (a pediatrician) emphasized these differences.[24] Recent studies utilizing psychological testing are now documenting these distinctions. Weeda-Mannak and Drop, of the Netherlands, compared ballet dancers

24. Druss, R. G. & Silverman, J. A. (1979), Body image and perfectionism of ballerinas: Comparison and contrast with anorexia nervosa, General Hospital Psychiatry, 2, 115–121.

(105 students from two national professional schools) with anorexia nervosa patients with respect to the following three psychological characteristics: the Drive to Achieve, the Motive to Avoid Failure (Negative Fear of Failure), and the Motive to Achieve (Positive Fear of Failure).[25] These researchers found that both ballet students and anorexia nervosa patients possessed a heightened Drive to Achieve compared with a control group, but the "desire to excel" in anorexia nervosa patients originated in an avoidance of failure (Negative Fear of Failure), while in the ballet students this drive was found to stem from a motive to achieve (Positive Fear of Failure).[26]

Druss and Silverman have commented upon this desire to excel:

> It is the wish to achieve a kind of perfectionism, the desire to do the thing perfectly and to achieve the special momentary bliss accompanying the perfectness, that motivates dancers. . . . It is a personal, self-directed state requiring no audience. Although an audience may one day approve and applaud, the experience for the dancer is essentially unsharable and intensely private. It has little to do with competition or fame, which also are secondary goals.[27]

Garner and coworkers, employing the EDI, have also demonstrated that exclusive emphasis on anorexic symptoms, without evaluation of psychological traits, may lead to the overdiagnosis or overidentification of anorexia nervosa. Ballet and university students were grouped into "weight-preoccupied" and "non weight-preoccupied" categories (on the basis of scores on the Drive for Thinness subscale), and compared with anorexia nervosa patients. The weight-preoccupied women could be divided into two subgroups; those with elevated scores on all eight subscales (considered to be indicative of significant eating pathology), and a larger group with elevated scores only on the Drive for Thinness, Body Dissatisfaction, and Perfectionism subscales (considered "normal dieters"). Thus, certain traits frequently observed in anorexia nervosa are relatively uncommon in weight-preoccupied women. The authors concluded that:

25. Hermans, H. J. M. (1970), A questionnaire measure of achievement motivation, *Journal of Applied Psychology, 54*, 353–363.

26. Weeda-Mannak, W. L. & Drop, M. J. (1985), The discriminative value of psychological characteristics in anorexia nervosa: Clinical and psychometric comparison between anorexia nervosa patients, ballet dancers, and controls. *Journal of Psychiatric Research, 19*, 285–290.

27. Druss, R. G. & Silverman, J. A., Body image and perfectionism of ballerinas, op. cit.

... although there are some highly weight-preoccupied females who display psychopathology quite similar to anorexia nervosa, others only superficially resemble patients suffering from serious eating disorders. These results underscore the importance of a multidimensional evaluation of psychopathology in those suspected of anorexia nervosa.[28]

Regardless of the terminology one prefers, early recognition and treatment of significant eating disorders must be given highest priority, since in the midst of "naturally thin" women, dancers with problems may be well camouflaged. Indeed, anorexic dancers typically hide behind the rationalization of the demand for the thinness in dance. Confronting the denial with professional help will serve these dancers well, since invariably their success in dance will be adversely affected by their eating problem. Drawing the line is never easy, but it is especially crucial that dance teachers, choreographers, administrators, and dancers themselves be aware of, and responsive to, these problems. All too often, the line is determined on a purely visual basis, as by the ballet scholarship student who told me:

> It's different for everybody. Each body looks differently; but I find it when a person is too thin to complete a graceful line, where the body gets to the point where it's angular instead of curved. When you look at the person and they don't look pleasing, that's the point.

As far as criteria go, this statement isn't particularly accurate or sensitive. Pleasing to whom? Who is going to decide? As Druss and Silverman have stated, dancers "have discovered an outlet through which seemingly deviant behavior is accepted, even rewarded." My feeling is that the dance world should neither promote, nor accept, "seemingly deviant behavior." The look, for obvious reasons, simply doesn't make it as a standard.

28.   Garner, D. M. et al., Comparison, op. cit.

6 Menstrual Themes and Variations

They don't menstruate . . . so what?

Lincoln Kirstein

My first exposure to the extent of menstrual irregularities in dancers came about quite inadvertently. An eighteen-year-old student from a ballet company school asked me a general question concerning vitamins. After I mentioned that she might select a multiple vitamin with supplemental iron—since menstrual flow accounts for increased iron losses—the dancer concluded, "Then I suppose my friends and I can just buy the kind without the extra iron."

The absence of menstrual periods caused little concern and had not been evaluated by a physician, simply because the dancer did not consider her irregularity at all unusual. In the residence house in which she lived with other dance students, periodicity seemed almost a novelty. Continuing my inquiries into the menstrual patterns of young dancers, I encountered a surprising number of girls who responded to "Do you have periods?" with a naive shrug or the more pat—though somewhat obtuse—reply:

"Yeah, sometimes."

Agnes de Mille has observed that "certain great soloists have been lacking in even primary sexual functions and are known to have menstruated rarely in their lives."[1] From talking to past generations of dancers, it does appear that menstrual irregularities were common, though, one would suppose, much less so than they are today. A former principal ballerina related the extensive medical testing she underwent—including a visit to a clinic in Switzerland—for evaluation of menstrual dysfunction and apparent infertility.

"Nothing worked," she told me, "I didn't have my periods except when we were on vacation. If we weren't performing for a couple of months, maybe then I would have it once. Nothing worked until I stopped performing and went into teaching." She is now the mother of three.

We might go back even farther—quite a way farther—to note that Aetius of Amida (the first eminent Christian physician of antiquity, who made house calls in the sixth century) made the observation that dancers do not menstruate. He also noted this of emaciated women, barren women, and pregnant women, as well as singers. For the entertainers, either of song or dance, he reasoned that the menstrual blood was consumed by too much exercise (the singers in those days must have done veritable Las Vegas acts).[2] But, conversely, many centuries before that, the reputable Hippocrates might have prescribed dancing as a cure for the failure to menstruate.[3]

Conflict and confusion about menstruation have abounded throughout the centuries; and naturally, men have made the most of their ignorance and dogmatism, with women bearing the brunt of the idiocies. Our medical predecessors were aware of the complexity and numerous contributing factors. Consider the shotgun approach of the early-nineteenth-century-physician Marc Colombat de L'Isère, whose diagnostic checklist for failure to menstruate included: living in a low, humid locality; lack of sunlight; want of exercise; insufficient nourishment; fatigue; anger; disappointed love; celibacy; despair; jealousy; immoderate joy; "depressing passions"; "vivid emotions of the soul"; reception of bad news; a sudden

---

1. de Mille, A. (1958), *And promenade home*, Boston: Little, Brown, p. 224.

2. Ricci, J. V. (1943), *The genealogy of gynaecology: History of the development of gynaecology throughout the ages*, Philadelphia: Blakiston, p. 194.

3. Dancing, Hippocrates believed, is beneficial for amenorrhea, as well as useful for inducing abortion.

fright; fear; sudden exposure to cold; the action of strong odors; ingestion of ices, sherbets, and cold drinks; and sitting on the grass, ground, or a stone bench.[4]

And if women dread visits to the gynecologists these days, a list of the elaborate and varied treatments of the past for failure to menstruate will leave them counting their blessings: fresh, dry air; nourishing food, particularly rich soups and roasts; wines and mineral waters (not bad so far); mineral-water douches; footbaths; hip baths; warm enemas; aromatic fumigations; fomentations to the external genitalia; cuppings to the thigh; bleedings from the extremities; and leeches to the vulva.[5] Verily, the modern physician is part of a great tradition of menstrual bewilderment.

By surveying aspiring ballet dancers in three highly competitive professional schools in New York City by questionnaire, I determined that only about one third of ballet students had regular menstrual cycles. A further analysis of this data, in conjunction with Drs. Rose Frisch and Grace Wyshak at Harvard Medical School, revealed that of eighty-nine dance students, 10 percent had not begun to menstruate by age sixteen (six of these were older than eighteen), 12 percent had not begun menstruating by fourteen years and four months, 15 percent had stopped menstruating once having started, and 30 percent had irregular cycles (leaving a third with regular cycles).[6] Subsequent studies have confirmed that only about one-third to one-half of ballet dancers have regular cycles (depending upon age and level of competitiveness).[7]

4.   Ricci, J. V. (1943), *The Genealogy of gynaecology*, op. cit., p. 519.

5.   Ibid., p. 521.

6.   Frisch, R. E., Wyshak, G., & Vincent, L. (1980), Delayed menarche and amenorrhea in ballet dancers, *New England Journal of Medicine, 303*, 17–19.

7.   See the following reports: Braisted, J. R., Mellin, L., Gong, E. J., & Irwin, C. E., Jr. (1985), The adolescent ballet dancer: Nutritional practices and characteristics associated with anorexia nervosa, *Journal of Adolescent Health Care, 6*, 365–371 [of the forty-five ballet students in San Francisco, 34 percent had not begun menstruating or had ceased to menstruate and 35 percent had irregular cycles]; Cohen, J. L., Kim, C. S., May, P. B., Jr., & Ertel, N. H. (1982), Exercise, body weight, and amenorrhea in professional ballet dancers, *The Physician and Sportsmedicine, 10*, 92–101 [of thirty-two professional dancers in a major company of international rank, 47 percent had a history of some type of menstrual dysfunction, 37 percent had a history of amenorrhea]; Calabrese, L. H., Kirkendall, D. T., Floyd, M., et al. (1983), Menstrual abnormalities, nutritional patterns, and body composition in female classical ballet dancers, *Physician and Sportsmedicine, 11*, 86–98 [of twenty-nine professional dancers and five scholarship students in a regional ballet company, 50 percent had some type of menstrual dysfunction]; Bright-See, E., Croy, J., Brayshaw, J., et al. (1978), Nutritional beliefs and practices of ballet students, *Journal of the Canadian Dietetic Association, 39*, 324–331 [of twenty-three students in a Canadian national ballet school, none between twelve and fourteen years had regular cycles, and only 50 percent of those over fourteen had regular cycles].

Among this group investigated by Drs. Frisch, Wyshak, and myself, the average age at which menstruation began (the mean age of menarche) was calculated at 13.7 years. Although significantly higher than the average age of menstrual onset for American girls in general (about 12.5 years), this figure was nonetheless a significant underestimate, since twenty of the eighty-nine girls had not yet menstruated and thus were not figured into the average. A more representative estimate of average age of menarche in a comparable group was reported by Dr. Michelle Warren, who followed fifteen serious ballet students in New York City for a four-year period and found a mean age of menarche of 15.4 years.[8] Other investigators have determined the mean age of menarche for ballet dancers to be slightly over 14 years, with menstrual onset occurring as late as 23 years of age.[9]

Because physicians experienced with dancers encounter menstrual difficulties so routinely, they have often been more conservative than others in their approach to the dysfunction. Since the irregularity may often be viewed as part and parcel of dancing, the doctor may take a wait-and-see posture, the only therapy being a bit of needed reassurance. (This approach is changing, given the potentially negative effects on bone mineral content, to be discussed in Chapter 8). In comforting dancers, one New York physician explained that every profession has its own problems, and in the case of ballet "the ovaries go to sleep."

Another physician used a less tranquil and more movement-oriented trope for his dancers, telling them, "Your body's moving one way, and your ovaries are moving another way, and there's bound to be a clash somewhere along the line."

Simplistic explanations but quaint, very quaint. Truthfully, I'm very supportative of personifying internal organs. Vividly can I visualize a yawning ovary, tucking itself into its pelvic omentum for a few winks, lulled by the soothing, rhythmic music of blood flowing through the inferior vena cava. Or another, after being bounced around in an anatomical

8. Warren, M. P. (1980), The effects of exercise on pubertal progression and reproductive function in girls, *Journal of Clinical Endocrinology and Metabolism, 51*, 1150–1157. Even this high figure is a slight underestimate, since Dr. Warren's average age of menarche does not include two dancers of eighteen who were still premenarchal at the time of her report.

9. See the following reports: Braisted, J. R., et al., The adolescent ballet dancer, op. cit. [forty-five ballet students in San Francisco had a mean age of menarche of 14.2 years]; Cohen et al., Exercise, body weight, and amenorrhea, op. cit. [thirty-two professional ballet dancers in a major company of international rank had a mean age of menarche of 14.2 years]; Calabrese, L., et al., Menstrual abnormalities, op. cit. [twenty-nine professional dancers and five scholarship students in a regional ballet company had a mean age of menarche of 14.3 years].

Waring blender (a lot of jumps in class), groping about to steady itself in a pulsating blur of dizziness, saying, "Phew, am I disoriented! Which way are the tubes?"

Certainly the metaphors serve their purpose, and resorting to them is arguably easier than explaining the intricacies of the menstrual cycle, a task that many doctors face with as much reluctance as the patient who has to listen and feign comprehension. A New York fertility expert—a skilled medical educator and writer—was attempting to explain the function of cervical mucous in response to a telephone question during a radio talk show. To simplify, he described the function of the secretions (which facilitate the transport of sperm to the ovum) as "putting out a welcome mat." A reasonable effort, I thought, but the moderator interrupted him promptly with, "Well, I don't think we should get too technical for our radio audience."

Since that time, I have often pondered "How technical is a welcome mat?" If it is, how on earth can one possibly talk about things like gonadotropin-releasing hormone or the hypothalamic-pituitary-ovarian axis to a group of dancers?

At any rate, to consider "amenorrhea" (failure to menstruate) or "oligomenorrhea" (few menstruations), one must first at least partially digest the basics of normal menstrual function. One need not be an endocrinologist to understand the major highlights and interrelationships. And, giving physiology a fighting chance, one becomes aware that the hormonal regulation of the female menstrual cycle is a fascinating and intricate piece of physiological choreography.

A Lesson In Female Reproductive Physiology

For many females, the bleeding phase of the menstrual cycle may be the only indication that the cycle is occurring. To make it clear that various parts of the body are working overtime all along, let us use menstruation as a convenient starting point for a brief general survey, beginning with the southernmost parts of the anatomy and working progressively north.

Menstrual blood represents a peeling off and shedding of part of the "endometrium," the lining of the uterus. Throughout the cycle, the uterine lining proliferates rapidly, increasing in thickness and vessel networks, developing glands for the production of secretions. The growth and changes are in preparation for the possible fertilization of an ovum and a readiness for pregnancy. Should pregnancy not occur, the beefed-up lining is sloughed, bleeding occurs, and the building-up process commences from scratch.

The changes in the wall of the uterus are controlled by the hormones estrogen and progesterone, both of which are produced by the ovaries. "Hormones" are chemical substances which have specific effects on a certain organ or "target." In this instance, then, the uterus is the target organ, and its activities and changes are influenced by, and dependent upon, the ovarian hormones. Hormones, in effecting body changes, might be viewed as signals—instructing, modulating, and integrating the communication of one part of the body to another.

The major function of progesterone is to prepare the endometrium for implantation of a fertilized egg and for the maintenance of pregnancy, and its effects are for the most part confined to the uterus. In a sense, it antagonizes the growth effects of estrogen, or rather, redirects the growth: estrogen stimulates the rapid growth of the endometrium, whereas progesterone stimulates the development of the uterine glands. In simple terms, estrogen affects the thickness of the lining, whereas progesterone affects the softness of the lining and its secretions, making the uterine wall conducive to implantation and support of the fertilized egg.

Estrogen, commonly regarded as the "female sex hormone," has a much broader job description. Aside from its effect on the uterine lining, it is responsible for many typical female characteristics. Breast growth and development, external female genitalia, the vaginal lining and secretions, and the deposition of body fat are all dependent on estrogen. The hormone also has a wide effect on general physiology, affecting blood proteins and fats, and exerting influence on the vascular and skeletal systems.

Just as the uterus responds to the hormonal secretions of the ovaries, the ovaries themselves are subservient to the secretions of the pituitary gland (they are the target organ for pituitary hormones). The "pituitary," about the size of a bean and located at the base of the skull, secretes multiple hormones which act on various targets for a variety of functions. For example, "thyroid stimulating hormone" (TSH) stimulates the development and function of the thyroid gland; "adrenocorticotropin" (ACTH) does the same for portions of the adrenal gland (which itself is concerned with the synthesis and secretion of hormones called "steroids"); "growth hormone" (GH) is essential for tissue growth and repair; and "prolactin" is concerned with lactation in females. But at present we are concerned with the two powerful pituitary hormones that circulate in the blood-stream to affect the ovaries. Together referred to as "gonadotropins," they include the "follicular stimulating hormone" (FSH) and "luteinizing hormone" (LH).

As its name implies, the function of FSH is to stimulate the growth of the "ovarian follicle" (the follicle includes the egg along with the cyst-like structure of cells that surround it, both serving to nourish and protect the ovum as it matures). LH is more responsible for the actual process of "ovulation," in which the "ripe" follicle is expelled from the ovary into the fallopian tube for possible fertilization by a sperm. The gonadotropins FSH and LH do not produce effects directly; rather some effects are determined by the type and relative amounts of the hormone secretions which they induce from the ovary (i.e., estrogen and progesterone).

Thus far we have traced the happenings in the uterus to the secretions of the ovary, which in turn result from secretions of the pituitary. The story does not end here, because the pituitary is controlled by a small section of the brain called the "hypothalamus." The hypothalamus (involved with such crucial matters as water balance, satiety, and regulation of the body's temperature) produces its own specialized hormones in nerve cells, so-called "releasing factors," which regulate the production and secretion of pituitary hormones. There are separate releasing factors for growth hormone, adrenocorticotropin, thyroid stimulating hormone, as well as FSH and LH. The releasing factor that controls the gonadotropins FSH and LH is called, originally enough, "gonadotropin-releasing hormone" (GnRH).

The higher up we go, the more complicated things become and the longer the names get. The crucial point to be aware of, however, is that the hypothalamus is the bridge connecting the nervous system (the brain) with the endocrine system (the body secretions). Since the hypothalamus in turn receives input from the higher centers of the brain, which in themselves are modified and influenced by the outside world, any number of factors from the internal as well as the external environment may affect the normal sequence of events. Influences such as sensory stimulation, emotional states, drugs, and hormone levels in the blood all may alter the hormone-secreting nerve cells of the hypothalamus, and hence the menstrual cycle.

The chain of command is more sophisticated than a strict superior-to-subordinate relationship. Unlike a one-way system, it is a circular one, integrated by a fine modulation of feedback, delicate hormonal signalings that may enhance or inhibit at various levels. For example, although the secretion of estrogen is the result of stimulation by FSH, high levels of estrogen shut off the production of FSH by the pituitary (negative feed-back). Conversely, higher levels of estrogen actually stimulate greater production of the other gonadotropin, LH (positive feedback). Not only do the ovarian hormones affect the secretion of hormones higher up the ladder (via messages to the hypothalamus); the gonadotropins may also influence their own production, as high levels of FSH and LH act on the hypothalamus to suppress their own releasing factors.

Thus, the ovaries may communicate with the hypothalamus, with posi-tive or negative instructions, as may the pituitary, and these lines of communication are referred to as "long" and "short feedback loops" (it's helpful to think of distances here; the ovaries are much farther from the hypothalamus than the pituitary is). The sum total of all of these interrela-tionships is termed the hypothalamic-pituitary-ovarian axis (Figure 21). Essentially, it's a system of checks and balances, insuring the integrity of the cycle. The alternative is a bunch of glands haphazardly doing their own thing, an undesirable situation when something so basic as propaga-tion of the species is at stake.

Given the remarkable control system regulating the menstrual cycle—dependent upon the synchronization and interrelationships of the hypo-thalamus, the pituitary, the ovaries, and the uterus—malfunctions may occur because of diseases involving the four principal players themselves or indirectly because of other disease states. An overactive thyroid, for instance, may interfere with the development of the endometrium indi-rectly, because excess thyroid hormone promotes rapid elimination of estrogen by the body. "Hepatitis," an inflammatory condition of the liver, may in some cases cause menstrual abnormalities via alterations in the normal metabolism of estrogen and progesterone. More pertinent to our discussion, though, will be the interplay of exercise, body composition, and stress factors.

The Hypothalamic-Pituitary-Ovarian Axis Encounters the Monkey Wrench

Now that we (hopefully) have the basics of reproductive physiology down pat, let's try to fit dancing and the exercising woman into the equation. Where along the line is menstrual functioning disrupted? For starters, dysfunction does not boil down simply to absent menstruation

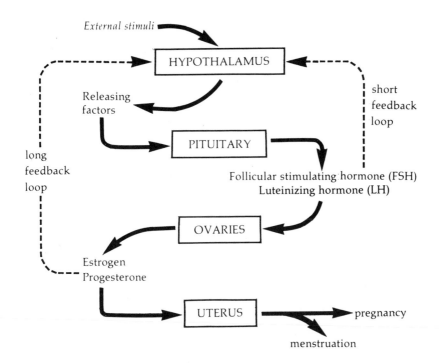

Figure 21. The hypothalamic-pituitary-ovarian axis

(amenorrhea) or intermittent menstruation (oligomenorrhea); difficulties among athletes may be more pervasive than actually appreciated because not all women who bleed at regular intervals have normal menstrual function. Menstrual patterns reveal only one aspect of the story.

For example, in a study of training marathon runners with apparently regular menses and no weight loss, two-thirds actually had cycle abnormalities (short luteal phase and anovulatory cycles, discussed below).[10] In another extremely well-designed prospective study, twenty-eight initially untrained college women with documented normal menstrual cycles underwent an eight-week progressive exercise program at a summer camp (consisting mainly of running, beginning at 4 miles and progressing

10. Prior, J. C., Cameron, K., Ho Yuen, B., & Thomas, J. (1982), Menstrual cycle changes with marathon training: Anovulation and short luteal phase, *Canadian Journal of Applied Sports Sciences*, 7, 173–177.

to 10 miles per day, but also including bicycling, tennis, or volleyball). The students were randomly assigned to weight-loss and weight-maintenance groups. Only four subjects (three in the weight-maintenance group) had a normal menstrual cycle during training, but all were again cycling normally within six months of the study's termination. Significantly, only 60 percent of the cycles were identifiable as abnormal by clinical assessment, whereas 89 percent were so characterized by hormonal measurements. The authors concluded that vigorous exercise, particularly if compounded by weight loss, can reversibly disturb reproductive function in women.[11]

Menstrual dysfunction in athletes may be broken down into three conditions, representing a progression of increasing severity.[12] With "luteal-phase deficiency," the portion of the menstrual cycle after ovulation (the luteal phase) is shorter than twelve days. This condition is often accompanied by reduced levels of progesterone and may be associated with infertility (the other two conditions are invariably associated with infertility). With "euestrogenic anovulation," ovulation does not occur; estrogen levels are normal but progesterone production is markedly decreased. (Normally, large quantities of progesterone are secreted following ovulation, and both estrogen and progesterone levels are high during the luteal phase.) The third condition, "hypoestrogenic amenorrhea," is a state of estrogen deficiency resulting from inadequate stimulation of the ovaries from higher centers.[13]

Low gonadotropin levels have been documented in many athletes, including dancers. The presence of low gonadotropin levels (despite normal or low steroid hormone levels, which would normally result in increased gonadotropins) is possibly the result of an inability of the hypo-

11. Bullen, B. A., Skrinar, G. S., Beitins, I. Z., et al., (1985), Induction of menstrual disorders by strenuous exercise in untrained women. *New England Journal of Medicine, 312*, 1349–1353.

12. Dr. Mona Shangold is an authority on the gynecologic problems of female athletes and has written many excellent original papers and review articles, including Shangold, M. (1982), Menstrual irregularity in athletes: Basic principles, evaluation, and treatment, *Canadian Journal of Applied Sports Science, 7*, 68–73; Shangold, M. (1985), Causes, evaluation, and management of athletic oligo-/amenorrhea, *Medical Clinics of North America, 69*, 83–95.

13. Two points of clarification here: (1) There are other, less frequent causes of menstrual dysfunction in women, which are not relevant to this discussion (but which must be excluded by the physician working up a patient with menstrual problems); and (2) a number of alterations in the levels of several other hormones and circulating blood proteins have been identified in athletes, among which are included prolactin, testosterone, cortisol, catecholamines, and opioid peptides. Consideration of these lines of investigation is well beyond the scope of this book, especially because the long-term effects, if any, of these alterations remain unclear.

thalamus to make or release gonadotropin-releasing-hormone (GnRH), a decreased pituitary sensitivity to this master hormone, or a desensitivity of the hypothalamus or pituitary to ovarian hormone levels (i.e., a malfunctioning of the feedback loop). In other words, the menstrual dysfunction of athletes involves the higher chain of command of the hypothalamic-pituitary-ovarian axis.

Because a multitude of factors influence reproductive function, and many variables can change simultaneously, determining the exact mechanism or mechanisms of menstrual dysfunction has been a sticky problem for endocrinologists and sports physiologists, and many areas of controversy remain. Consider the following quote from a review article entitled "Does Exercise Training Affect Reproductive Hormones in Women?":

> A plethora of hypothetical mechanisms have been proposed to explain the wide range of often dubious hormonal measurements made under a wide variety of conditions in disparate types of subjects. None of these mechanisms can be regarded as demonstrated, and contrary evidence has been raised against most.[14]

Fortunately we don't not need to get totally bogged down in the mire to explore some general, well-established interrelationships between dancing/exercise and menstrual dysfunction. As summed up by Dr. Shangold:

> During the course of any training program an athlete is subjected to not only the exercise itself, but also any or all of the following: the physical stress of training, the emotional stress of training and/or competing, weight loss, low weight, loss of body fat, and low body fat. Each of these, alone or in combination, may contribute to the development of menstrual irregularity or amenorrhea.[15]

In the next section, we shall attempt to isolate and explore these factors.

---

14.   Loucks, A. B. (1986), Does exercise training affect reproductive hormones in women? *Clinics in Sports Medicine, 5,* 535–557. Things aren't quite that bleak, since Anne Loucks concedes that "the few studies less susceptible to such criticism are consistent in their observations of gonadotropin and ovarian steroid suppression in women participating in athletic training."

15.   Shangold, M., Menstrual irregularity in athletes, op. cit.

The Triggering of Menarche:
The Frisch Hypothesis

Before periods can become irregular or disappear altogether, they have to be present in the first place. So it makes perfect sense to begin our exploration of dancing and menstrual dysfunction at the beginning of menstruation, or menarche. The first of several case histories (the histories are factual, only the names are fictitious) will serve as our hypothetical model.

> *Case 1*: Sara is a nineteen-year-old scholarship student in a New York City ballet company school. She began dancing at the age of six, has been studying seriously since age twelve, and has not yet menstruated. She is five feet, six inches in height, and weighs 90 pounds.

Provided that there is no physical abnormality accounting for her initial failure to menstruate ("primary amenorrhea"), Sara might simply be called a "late bloomer." Obviously she is well behind schedule, since we have already learned that the current average age of menarche in the United States is roughly twelve-and-a-half years. A hundred years ago, though, Sara's case would have appeared less striking, as in those days menarche occurred most commonly at fifteen or sixteen. In a study of four thousand females in England in 1848, only 494 had begun to menstruate before the age of thirteen years and eight months and 632 did not begin until approximately their eighteenth birthday or later.[16] This trend toward earlier menarche (approximately two to three months earlier per decade in the past century-and-a-half in Europe; about two months per decade in the past century in the United States) is consistent with the well-documented acceleration of height and weight of girls and boys over the past hundred years and with the fact that menarche is delayed by undernutrition and strenuous physical exercise.[17]

Is Sara undernourished? Regardless of the beauty of her ballet line— whether or not one would consider her "slender," "skinny," or "too skinny"—the research of Dr. Rose Frisch and her coworkers over nearly

16.   Whitehead, J. (1848), *On the causes and treatment of abortion and sterility*, Philadelphia: Lea & Blanchard, p. 61.

17.   Wyshak, G. & Frisch, R. E. (1982), Evidence for a secular trend in age of menarche, *New England Journal of Medicine, 306*, 1033–1035.

two decades suggests that Sara and other young dancers like her are just too thin to start menstruating.

The Frisch hypothesis, which explains the effect of malnutrition on menarche as well as the trend for an earlier menarche, postulates a direct relationship between a critical "fatness" and the onset of menstruation. Through statistical investigations, it was found that the mean weight of early and late-maturing girls (about 106 pounds) does not differ at menarche, although the girls who menstruate at a late age are significantly taller.[18] In other words, early maturers have more weight per height than their late-maturing counterparts. Subsequent data supported the notion that the ratio of body fat to lean body mass is important in determining sexual maturation. For the onset of menstruation, it was hypothesized that a minimum of approximately 17 percent of the total body weight must be fat.[19]

Table 7 includes the ages, heights, and weights of twenty ballet students in New York City who have not yet undergone menarche. I have plotted these heights and weights on a chart (Figure 22) devised by Drs. Frisch and McArthur, in which diagonal lines indicate approximate percentages of fat relative to total body weight. (The lines represent percentiles of the ratio of total body water to lean body weight, an indicator of "relative fatness)". Seven of the girls (including Sara) are at or below the level of body fat considered by Dr. Frisch to be necessary for the onset of menstruation. Thus, we might speculate, in accordance with the Frisch hypothesis, that Sara and her six classmates have not yet menstruated because they don't possess a large enough percentage of body fat. Sara would have to gain about 9 pounds to reach the minimum weight for menarche.

But what about the other thirteen girls? Indeed, they have surpassed the minimum fat content, yet still they haven't begun their periods. The key point here is that the Frisch hypothesis proposes that the minimum fatness is necessary, but not sufficient, for the initiation of menstruation. That is, while menstruation should not occur below the minimum fat threshold, other factors (such as emotional or physical stress) may interfere with menstrual onset even though the threshold has been reached. The age at which females initiate training may be a factor; in a study of

---

18. Frisch, R. E. & Revelle, R. (1971), Height and weight at menarche and a hypothesis of menarche, *Archives of Disease in Childhood, 46,* 695–701.

19. Frisch, R. E. & McArthur, J. W. (1974), Menstrual cycles: Fatness as a determinant of minimum weight for height necessary for their maintenance or onset, *Science, 185,* 949–951.

Table 7.   Age, Height, and Weight of Twenty Students of Ballet in New York City Who Have Never Had a Menstrual Period

Age	Height	Weight (pounds)
12	5′1″	85
13	5′ 4″	90
13	5′1/2″	82
13	5′	85
14	5′ 21/2″	96
15	5′ 31/2″	100
15	5′ 11/2″	90
15	5′ 41/2″	101
15	5′ 4″	95
15	5′ 21/2″	95
16	5′ 4″	98
16	5′ 41/2″	97
17	5′ 21/2″	95
18	5′ 5″	95
18	5′ 6″	90*
18	5′ 31/2″	97
19	5′ 41/2″	95
19	5′ 2″	95
20	5′ 51/2″	102
20	5′ 61/2″	95

*Sara

athletes trained before and after menarche (swimmers and runners), each year of training before menarche was found to delay menarche by five months, possibly a reflection of body composition or perhaps representing an independent effect of training upon the menstrual cycle.[20]

We should remember that genetic factors, not just environmental ones, influence the age of menarche. Are we perhaps attributing too much to environmental influences here? Available evidence suggests not. In a recent survey of 350 adolescent dancers and other girls and their mothers, the dancers had a later age of menarche, while the age of menarche of the mothers did not differ. In nondancers, the maternal menarchal age was the best predictor of age of menstrual onset for the daughters, while the degree of leanness was the best predictor of menarchal age in the dancers.

20.   Frisch, R. E., Gotz-Welbergen, A. V., McArthur, J. W., et al. (1981), Delayed menarche and amenorrhea of college athletes in relation to age of onset of training, *Journal of the American Medical Association*, 246, 1559–1563.

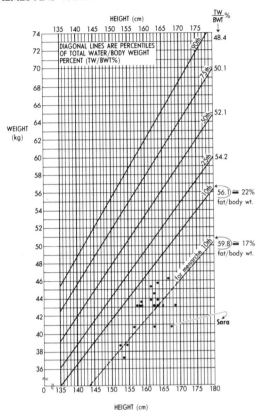

Figure 22. "Relative fatness" as related to menstrual onset (Reprinted by permission of Rose E. Frisch. Chart published in Frisch, R. E. & McArthur, J. W. (1974), Menstrual cycles: Fatness as a determinant of minimum weight for height necessary for their maintenance or onset, *Science, 185,* 949–951. Copyright © 1974 by the American Association for the Advancement of Science)

These results sugggest that delayed menarche in dancers is not principally attributable to genetic factors.[21]

Menstrual Maintenance

Our next three case histories involve young women who have menstruated, but who have either stopped or now menstruate intermittently. Their

21. Brooks-Gunn, J. & Warren, M. P. (1988), Mother-daughter differences in menarcheal age in adolescent girls attending national dance company schools and nondancers, *Annals of Human Biology, 15,* 35–44.

stories will serve to illustrate the additional potential interrelationships of weight loss and body composition on the menstrual cycle.

> *Case 2*: Susan, a nineteen-year-old student of ballet, had her first menstrual period at twelve, but has not menstruated at all for almost three years. Her weight at the time of her last period was in the neighborhood of one hundred pounds; her height, five-feet, four-inches. Subsequently, she lost a total of 10 pounds, and continues to dance at 90 pounds, a weight with which she is happy.

Susan exemplifies a condition termed "secondary amenorrhea," or cessation of menstruation after menarche has occurred (as opposed to primary amenorrhea, the failure of menses to appear by the age of eighteen). Just as undernourishment delays the onset of menstruation, it can stop menstruation altogether. In fact, simple weight loss per se is enough to result in dysfunction of the hypothalamus, thus affecting the secretion of gonadotropins by the pituitary and ultimately affecting levels of estrogen and other hormones.[22] Low body weight in females may also correlate with abnormalities in the regulation of body temperature and convervation of body water. (In the extreme emaciation of anorexia nervosa, more severe and extensive hormonal changes occur, many if not all of them consequences of nutritional deprivation.)

Clearly, nutrition is of prime importance in hormonal regulation; the human female needs adequate energy stores to meet the increased demands of pregnancy and lactation. Researchers investigating the Sans tribes in Africa have demonstrated a seasonal variation in fertility according to variations in nutritional status among this hunting and gathering population.[23] And although it is commonly believed that malnourished populations have high fertility rates, this is not the case. (The issue is often clouded by the absence of contraception in underdeveloped nations.) In India, for instance, the mean interval between pregnancies in low-income groups—in which contraceptive practices are not employed—is thirty-two months. Factors accounting for this interval include delayed puberty (diminishing the years of reproductive ability), decreased

22. Vigersky, R. A., Andersen, A. E., Thompson, R.H., et al. (1977), Hypothalamic dysfunction in secondary amenorrhea associated with simple weight loss, *New England Journal of Medicine, 297*, 1141–1145.

23. Wilmsen, E. N. (1978), Seasonal effects of dietary intake on Kalahari San, *Federation Proceedings, 37*, 65–72; van der Walt, L. A., Wilmsen, E. N., & Jenkins, T. (1978), Unusual sex hormone patterns among desert-dwelling hunter-gatherers, *Journal of Clinical Endocrinology and Metabolism, 46*, 658–663.

potential fertility (amenorrhea without ovulation), extended breast feeding (ovulation is much less frequent among women who nurse their
infants than among those who do not), a greater number of miscarriages,
and a higher percentage of maternal mortality and stillbirths.[24] Clearly,
malnourishment is a principal player here.

Dieting (even in the absence of strenuous exercise) may result in the subtle
and not-so-subtle changes in the menstrual cycle that we've previously
discussed in connection with athletes. Of nine normally menstruating
young women who dieted for six weeks (consuming 800–1,000 kcal per
day, and losing roughly between 13 and 18 pounds), no ovulation occurred in six subjects during the dieting period, and the menstrual periods
of two women (who began the study with anovulatory cycles) were
disrupted.[25] More recently, to evaluate whether short-term energy deprivation affects sex hormone patterns, six healthy women were studied
over two menstrual cycles. Energy intake during the first cycle was
designed to keep body weight constant, but was reduced by 41 percent in
the second cycle. Weight loss ranged from roughly 7 to 14 pounds during
the low energy diet, and two of the leannest women (who also lost the
most weight) became anovulatory and amenorrheic. The principal difference between these two women and the others was in body composition.[26]

Although Susan is not an anorexic, Mother Nature may nonetheless
view her as malnourished (insofar as she might not be a particularly good
reproductive risk). Her menstrual dysfunction (and that of the others)
might thus be looked upon as physiologic or adaptive.

Case 3: Lynn is an eighteen-year-old ballet dancer who began menstruating regularly at thirteen, began dancing seriously at fourteen-
and-a-half, and currently menstruates about three or four times a
year. She is five-feet, five-inches in height and weighs 106 pounds.

Case 4: Margaret is twenty years old, is five-feet, five-inches in
height, and has irregular periods. She weighs approximately 110
pounds, and has observed that she hardly ever menstruates when she
is below that weight.

Both of these young women manifest "oligomenorrhea," a reduction
in the frequency of the menses (technically, the diagnosis is indicated if

24. Gopalan, C. & Naidu, A. N. 1972. Nutrition and fertility, *Lancet, 2,* 1077–1078.

25. Pirke, K. M., Schweiger, U., Lemmel, W., et al. (1985), The influence of dieting on the
menstrual cycle of healthy young women, *Journal of Clinical Endocrinology and Metabolism, 60,*
1174–1179.

26. Kurzer, M. S. & Calloway, D. H. (1986), Effects of energy deprivation on sex hormone
patterns in healthy menstruating women, *American Journal of Physiology, 251,* E483-E488.

the intervals are longer than thirty-eight days but shorter than three months). I have already alluded to the theorized relationship between body composition and menstrual onset. Let's consider fatness in this slightly different context by referring again to the work of Dr. Rose Frisch.

Just as a critical amount of body fat is proposed as necessary for menarche, Dr. Frisch has convincingly hypothesized that established menstrual function ceases in older girls when fat levels fall below about 22 percent of body weight. In the female over sixteen who has already menstruated but has stopped because of weight loss or low weight, approximately this amount of fat (more accurately, leanness as determined by the ratio of body water to total weight) is indicated as the minimum for the restoration and maintenance of menstrual cycles.[27] This target body composition is again "necessary, but not sufficient," as other factors may prevent normal reproductive functioning, irrespective of "fatness."

From Figure 23, another "relative fatness" graph, we see that when the heights and weights of Lynn and Margaret are plotted, they fall very close to the critical diagonal for menstrual maintenance. We can also see that Susan (Case 2), amenorrheic for nearly three years, is well below the critical threshold (in fact, she is even below the even lower minimum required for onset of menstruation). We might speculate that the fatness levels of Lynn and Margaret are not adequate to maintain regular cycles. That Margaret is herself aware of a critical "weight" (this is not at all unusual for dancers, I've found) correlates very nicely with the observation that she is hovering at the borderline of minimal body fat necessary for regularity.

Because we've come this far with fat, I'll round off the discussion with a brief summary of ways in which the amount of body fat could conceivably influence reproductive function:[28]

1. Fatty tissue (and not just sex organs) can produce estrogen (by converting androgens to estrogen); thus, low body fat could potentially decrease total estrogen available.[29]
2. Body fat can store steroid hormones, which might influence hormonal regulatory mechanisms.

27. Frisch, R. E. & McArthur, J. W. (1974), Menstrual cycles, op. cit.

28. Frisch, R. E. (1987), Body fat, menarche, fitness and fertility, *Human Reproduction, 2,* 521–533; Frisch, R. E. (1988, March), Fatness and fertility, *Scientific American,* 88–95.

29. Nimrod, A. & Ryan, K. J. (1975), Aromatization of androgens by human abdominal and breast fat tissue, *Journal of Clinical Endocrinology and Metabolism, 40,* 367–372; Frisch, R. E., Canick, J. A., & Tulchinsky, D. (1980), Human fatty marrow aromatizes androgen to estrogen, *Journal of Clinical Endocrinology and Metabolism, 51,* 394–396.

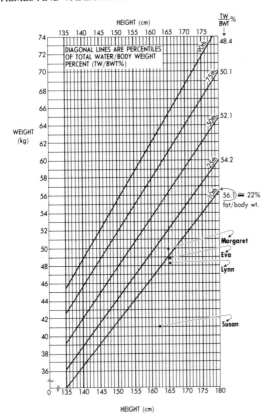

Figure 23. "Relative fatness" as related to maintenance of normal menstrual function. Reprinted by permission of Rose E. Frisch. Chart published in Frisch, R. E. & McArthur, J. W., Menstrual cycles, op. cit. Copyright © 1974 by the American Association for the Advancement of Science.)

3. Body weight and fatness influence the type of estrogen produced, with underweight women producing relatively more of a less potent form (the catechol estrogen, "2-hydroxyestrone," as opposed to "estradiol"). Not only does 2-hydroxyestrone have less biological activity than estradiol, it might interfere with neurotransmitter ("catecholamine") metabolic pathways and thus alter the regulation of gonadotropin release.[30]

4. Fatness is associated with a diminished capacity of serum "sex-hormone binding globulin" (SHBG), which results in a higher amount of estrogen circulating in the unbound state. Leaner

30. Fishman, J., Boyar, R. M., & Hellman, L. (1975), Influence of body weight on estradiol metabolism in young women, *Journal of Clinical Endocrinology and Metabolism, 41,* 989–991; Whitworth, N. S., & Meeks, G. R. (1985), Hormone metabolism: Body weight and extraglandular estrogen production, *Clinical Obstetrics and Gynecology, 28,* 580–587.

women, on the other hand, have a higher binding capacity, and thus less free-circulating estrogen.[31]

5. Low fat levels may alter temperature control or energy metabolism, affecting hypothalamic responses.

The notion of a specific critical fatness level applicable to entire populations (i.e., 17 percent of total body weight for menstrual onset, 22 percent for menstrual maintenance) has been challenged, although relatively little reliable hard data is available to substantiate this position, let alone to present a specific alternative hypothesis.[32] While not denying the important role of body fat, some investigators hypothesize that each individual has her own particular threshold,[33] that adaptations may ultimately override a specific threshold, that fat levels are reflective of metabolic triggering by other mechanisms, or that menstrual function is dependent on relative fat deposition in certain body sites.[34]

I anticipate continued debate and conflicting reports in this area for some time because: (1) the confounding influences of physical and emotional stresses upon the menstrual cycle make it difficult to examine body composition in isolation; (2) regular monthly bleeding does not exclude menstrual dysfunction (thus, assessment of cycle normalcy must include hormonal, not just clinical, assessment); (3) absolute body estimations vary widely, depending on the method of determination (skinfold thickness measurements, hydrostatic weighing, mathematical equations).[35] Thus, evidence refuting the Frisch hypothesis that is based on the obser-

31.   Nisker, J. A., Hammond, G. L., & Siiteri, P. K. (1980), More on fatness and reproduction (Letter to the Editor), *New England Journal of Medicine, 303,* 1124.

32.   Loucks, A. B. & Horvath, S. M. (1985), Athletic amenorrhea: A review, *Medicine and Science in Sports and Exercise, 17,* 56–72; Scott, E. C. & Johnston, F. E. (1982), Critical fat, menarche, and the maintenance of menstrual cycles: A critical review, *Journal of Adolescent Health Care, 2,* 249–260.

33.   Carlberg, K. A., Buckman, M. T., Peake, G. T., & Riedesel, M. L. (1983), Body composition of oligo/amenorrheic athletes, *Medicine and Science in Sports and Exercise, 15,* 215–217.

34.   Brownell, K. D., Steen, S. N., & Wilmore, J. H. (1987), Weight regulation practices in athletes: Analysis of metabolic and health effects, *Medicine and Science in Sports and Exercise, 19,* 546–556.

35.   Frisch, R. E. (1985), Body composition in amenorrheic athletic women (Letter to the Editor), *Annals of Internal Medicine, 103,* 153; Frisch, R. E. (1985), Weighing the evidence (Letter to the Editor), *The Lancet, 2,* 952.

vation of "normal" menstruation below "specific" body fat percentages must be carefully scrutinized.[36]

The Stresses of Dancing

That undernourishment and diminished body fat contribute to a goodly number of menstrual difficulties encountered in the dance world seems straightforward. However, Charles Darwin's observation that "hard living . . . retards the period at which animals conceive,"[37] encompasses more than the obvious restraints imposed on fertility by poor nutrition. Well accepted, and long a part of folklore and common observation, is the interruption of the menstrual cycle occurring as the result of environmental stresses or changes. And here one cannot rely on the statistical security of points and lines on a chart. We have already seen that strenuous exercise, apart from body weight and fat, influences menstrual function. Emotional stresses, such as moving away from home, competition in a company school, or the pressures of a performing season, are sufficient disruptions in themselves.[38] Attempting to separate the physical from emotional stresses of dancing is a fruitless endeavor.

Consider the not unusual situation illustrated by our last two case histories:

36.   As an example, consider two studies in which mean body fat percentages were not significantly different between menstrual cycling and noncycling athletes: Sanborn, C. F., Albrecht, B. H., & Wagner, W. W., Jr. (1987), Athletic amenorrhea: Lack of association with body fat, *Medicine and Science in Sports and Exercise, 19,* 207–212; Marcus, R., Cann, C., & Madvig, P., et al. (1985), Menstrual function and bone mass in elite women distance runners: Endocrine and metabolic features, *Annals of Internal Medicine, 102,* 158–163. As well, in the Marcus study the percent of body fat of all of the subjects was calculated by hydrostatic weighing to be substantially below 22 percent of body weight for all women (in fact, all but one subject had less than 17 percent body fat). Out of curiosity, I plotted the subjects from both studies on the Frisch nomogram. Interestingly enough, all of the menstruating women, despite computed absolute values for body fat, end up above the critical diagonal, while nearly half of the noncycling women are at or below the threshold diagonal.

37.   Darwin, C. (1868), *The variation of animals and plants under domestication,* London: John Murray, Vol. 2, p. 112.

38.   In a study of menstrual patterns of healthy girls in an independent high school, all girls whose cycles changed from regular to irregular (sixteen out of eighteen) were boarding students, separated from family and familiar surroundings. See Wilson, C., Emans, S. J., Mansfield, J., et al. (1984), The relationships of calculated percent body fat, sports participation, age, and place of residence on menstrual patterns in healthy adolescent girls at an independent New England high school, *Journal of Adolescent Health Care, 5,* 248–253.

Case 5: Eva is a twenty-six year old ballet instructor in New York City, who characteristically menstruates only during vacations from her dancing schedule. Her weight remains more or less constant at 107 pounds, her height is five-feet, five-inches.

Case 6: Kathy, an eighteen-year-old ballet scholarship student, had to curtail her dancing schedule for two months owing to a back injury. During that time, she menstruated for the first time. Her weight of approximately 92 pounds (her height is five-feet, two-and-a-half-inches) has not varied appreciably over the past few months.

In both instances, the abatement of dancing affected menstrual activity, resulting in resumption of periods in the former case, and initiation of periods in the latter. When Eva's height and weight are plotted in Figure 22, we see that she is near the minimum postulated weight for maintenance of regular cycles. Perhaps her body composition changes during vacation without a change in weight (relatively more fat and less lean body mass) and the critical-fatness hypothesis still holds. On the other hand, Eva's menstrual irregularity may be more directly related to the stress of dancing. This stress may arise from the physical demands of strenuous exercise (in some manner related to changes in body metabolism caused by increased work and energy demands), or from mental strain and pressure, or from both.

Dr. Michelle Warren has described cases of dancers similar to Eva and Kathy, in which the onset of menarche (or the resolution of secondary amenorrhea) correlated with a decrease in exercise and/or injury forcing rest of at least a two-month duration. During this interval, weight gain was minimal or absent. The normalizing of menstrual function, most notably in dancers with a lower body fat, appeared to be associated with "discontinuation of the energy drain."[39] Abraham et al., also observing that menstrual regularity of ballet students improved during periods of injury and long vacation, concluded that deterioration of the menstrual pattern during dancing periods was related to strenuous physical exercise rather than to any change in body weight.[40] Other investigators have noted increased dancing-induced menstrual irregularity or off-season regularity.[41]

39.   Warren, M. P., The effects of exercise on pubertal progression, op. cit.

40.   Abraham, S. F., Beumont, P. J. V., Fraser, I. S., & Llewellyn-Jones, D. (1982), Body weight, exercise and menstrual status among ballet dancers in training, *British Journal of Obstetrics and Gynaecology, 89,* 507–510.

41.   Cohen, et al., Exercise, body weight, and amenorrhea, op. cit.; Calabrese, et al., Menstrual abnormalities, op. cit.

Certainly the physical demands and emotional pressures on dancers are as great or greater than those of other female athletes, while the professional necessity for a low percentage of body fat, particularly in the classical dancer, is much greater than in most other disciplines. Granted, the variables are multitudinous, the physiological system is complex, and individual variability is great. Still, we may comfortably accept at least one straightforward, causal relationship: Thinness—in and of itself or along with the stresses of dancing—may be responsible for both the delay in the onset of menstruation and the lack of maintenance of a regular menstrual cycle.

Menstruation and Performance

The incidence of menstrual dysfunction among dancers is difficult to assess. The previous discussion, focusing primarily on a susceptible group, may not necessarily accurately depict the dance population in its entirety. Even among the aspiring ballet dancers surveyed, a third had completely regular periods. I suspect that a general survey of all dancers, including more mature ballet dancers, regional ballet dancers, and jazz and modern dancers, would reveal a lesser frequency of menstrual problems (though possibly still significantly greater than a control group of nondancing, nonathlete females). For the majority of dancers, then, the concern may not be menstruating per se, but dealing with symptoms that might accompany the cycle.

I have already alluded to physiological changes that occur as a result of hormone shifts. High levels of estrogen not only increase water retention, but also effect subtle changes in the permeability of small blood vessels, metabolism, and body temperature. It has been suggested that certain women might be more active because of peak estrogen levels. Some female athletes report that they perform best immediately after menstruation, relatively well in the middle of the cycle, and most poorly during menstruation, particularly the first two days. In one study, however, 46 percent reported no significant difference.[42]

Whatever the differences, the implication is that physical performance is not altered dramatically by hormonal nuances; the menstrual cycle appears to have minor influence upon the athletic performance of most

42. Albohm, M. (1976), Does menstruation affect performance in sports?, *Physician and Sports-medicine, 4,* 76–78.

competitors.[43] Perhaps slight changes in efficiency may be discernible to a dancer keenly attuned to her physicality; water retention and cramping, however, are not easily overlooked.

"Dysmenorrhea," or pain associated with menstruation, is a poorly understood condition, partially because of the subjective nature of the symptoms. Sports and strenuous activity can have both favorable and unfavorable effects on symptoms. It is generally assumed that females involved in regular exercise have fewer problems with menstrual pain and cramping, the exception being swimmers, in whom many investigators feel the prevalence of dysmenorrhea to be higher. In any event, the symptoms which arise, if any, as well as the attitude and reaction toward these symptoms, will vary with the individual.

There is little evidence that training or performing during menstruation can unfavorably affect the cycle. Certainly, neither world-class athletes nor dancers are going to avoid training or performing because of irregularity or discomfort. Full participation in dance should be allowed at all phases of the menstrual cycle; the final decision of whether or not to perform should always rest with the dancer.

Most major ballet companies in America have a contract clause allowing their dancers time off for menstrual discomfort. Similarly, dancers in Russia have been guaranteed the option of three days off a month to accommodate menstrual symptoms, by order of the office of the minister of culture.[44] I learned in an interview with a Russian ballerina that—as in this country—most of the dancers are able to dance throughout the month. Nevertheless, a number of Russian dancers, particularly the corps girls, take advantage of the three-day allowance to obtain a needed rest from their grueling schedule.

Perhaps this provision for calling in sick seems a luxury to corps members in this country. I find it hard to imagine a promising young dancer in a major company, working hard for solo roles and facing stiff competition from her colleagues at the *barre,* approaching a choreographer with, "I think I'll skip class and the performance tonight. You know, it's that time of the month, and I feel a bit out of sorts."

At first glance, the three-day allowance in Russia seems quite sympathetic and considerate, but even the best intentions may be perverted. A physician associated with the ballet world in Russia, who subsequently

---

43. Eston, R. G. (1984), The regular menstrual cycle and athletic performance, *Sports Medicine,* *1,* 431–445.

44. I heard this originally from two different Russian ballet dancers; it was corroborated by a physician associated with the ballet in Russia.

emigrated to the United States, told me a disheartening anecdote. A principal ballerina, known to have incapacitating menstrual symptomatology, did not see eye to eye with the artistic director of her company. By more than mere coincidence, her schedule worked out in such a way that her major performances nearly always coincided with the menstrual phase of her cycle. As a result, she missed performances because of "illness," a fact exploited by the director when appealing to the cultural ministry for her dismissal.

Dancers are disciplined and accustomed to dealing with professional adversity, be it from bleeding feet, aching muscles, an injury, or menstrual symptoms. How can one who transcends emotions and physicality be brought down to earth by the "monthlies"? The general consensus is that the dancer who misses performances because of menstrual problems is definitely the exception. Often, those that feel ill in the morning find they can work through their discomfort by taking class.

Of course, being a trooper doesn't make the problems disappear. If one were to talk exclusively with aspiring ballet dancers in New York and dancers burdened with a variety of menstrual complaints, one might conclude that there are two groups of dancers: those who have amenorrhea, and those who don't but wish they did. I recall an interview with a principal dancer on one of her "rotten days." For her, the ramifications of the premenstrual period and days of bleeding were boundless. Aside from the depression, irritability, and cramping she experienced, her dancing technique was noticeably hampered. Fluid retention and swollen breasts threw her off balance during multiple pirouettes and required compensating adjustments. From the sound of it, she was a monthly walking disaster area.

"Have you ever missed a performance because of your period?" I asked. (Her career had already extended over twenty years.)

"Never," she said. She looked at me as if to say, "What a stupid question."

7 Developing as Dancers and Women: Peter Pan On Pointe

Very few dancers develop the bodies of mature women; they keep lean in the hips and flat-breasted, a phenomenon remarked on by all costume designers. It is also a fact that the greatest performers, the women best capable of communicating sensuous satisfaction, are in their bodies the least sensual. In effect they have sacrificed all organs of personal fulfillment and maintain and cherish only the means for public satisfaction, the system of bones and sinews for levitation and propulsion.

Agnes de Mille, *And Promenade Home*

I'm a dancer first, before anything else, so I have to look like a dancer.

Member, New York City Ballet

Perhaps Agnes de Mille leaps into the orchestra pit with her generalization, but one doesn't have to be a costume designer to know that most dancers, particularly those in classical ballet, are lean in the hips and flat-breasted. Nothing profound here, but I'll summarize the obvious explanation anyway: (1) from an early age, aspiring ballerinas will not be accepted into professional company schools if they are heavy or appear to have that tendency; (2) technically skilled dancers, if heavy, will fare poorly in ballet-company auditions; and (3) dancers in companies who become heavy will either reduce or relocate. Conclusion: dance "selects for" thin women. This explains why, after paying a pretty penny for orchestra seats at Lincoln Center, the San Francisco Opera House, or any other ballet house, you do not often see women dancers with legs that look like sausage rolls.

That line of reasoning is hard to dispute, but it tells only part of the story, since selection in dance is a two-way street (maybe more like a busy thoroughfare, but we'll postpone the traffic jam of selection until the last chapter). Assuredly, the ideal dance body may be born, but it may also, at least in part, be created. Specifically, the dance has the capacity to delay and modify an individual's physical development, preserving the linear, adolescent body form so well suited to aesthetic and performance values in dance.

This statement is not such a big jump from relationships brought out in the previous chapter. We have seen that the stresses of dancing alone or combined with thinness may delay the onset of menstruation or affect it once it has occurred. Menstruation, though, is not an isolated phenomenon, as it reflects hormonal influences that may have other manifestations. And it's precisely these other manifestations that may determine the body configuration of a dancer.

A Lesson in "Natural" Female Development

Puberty refers to the transitional phase of development, the period of limbo bridging childhood and full maturity. The limbo is far from haphazard, and although the causes of the onset of puberty are enormously complicated and incompletely understood, there is a well-recognized order of progression. Menarche is really a late event in this physiological evolution, so let's identify the other components of puberty that end in "arche" (Greek for "beginning") before putting it all together.[1]

1. For this discussion, I have relied primarily on Brisson, G. R., Dulac, S., Péronnet, F., & Ledoux, M. (1982), The onset of menarche: A late event in pubertal progression to be affected by

"Adrenarche" (etymologically, the combination of "adrenal" with "arche"), the first in the series of events, occurs between the ages six and eight and corresponds to an increase in release of hormones from the adrenal gland.

"Gonadarche" ("gone" is from the Greek for "seed") designates the time frame (about age ten) when the hypothalamic-pituitary-ovarian axis becomes activated. This corresponds to the initiation of the growth spurt.

"Thelarche" ("thele" is Greek for "nipple") marks the beginning of breast development. The complete process normally takes three to four years and consists of five stages (Marshall and Tanner's classification).[2] The development of the breasts is primarily under the control of estrogens secreted by the ovaries.

"Pubarche," which chronologically follows thelarche by a few months, refers to the appearance of pubic and axillary hair (starting at about age eleven), which requires approximately three years for full development (and also is divided into five distinct stages). Hair growth is mainly under the control of androgens secreted by the ovary and the adrenal.

Finally we come to menarche, at about twelve-and-a-half for non-dancing U.S. girls. Although breast buds and pubic hair may appear two to three years before the first period, actual enlargement of the breasts and growth of the pelvis (including the accumulation of fat on the hips that contributes to the normal female contour) do not really get under way until approximately one year after menarche.

Ordinarily, the adolescent growth spurt reaches its peak at about two months before menarche, then steadily declines and is virtually completed within one to three years after the first period. Between the start of the growth spurt and menarche, by far the greatest component of weight gain is fat: body fat increases by about 125 percent (from an average of roughly 11 pounds at growth-spurt initiation to about 25 pounds at menarche), compared to an average 42 percent increase in lean body mass (muscle).[3] The priming of the ovaries for reproductive function,

physical training, *Canadian Journal of Applied Sport Sciences 7*, 61–67; and Styne, D. M. & Grumback, M. M. (1986), Puberty in the male and female: Its physiology and disorders, in S. S. C. Yen & R. B. Jaffe (eds.), *Reproductive endocrinology: Physiology, pathophysiology and clinical management*. New York: W. B. Saunders, pp. 313–384.

2.   Marshall, W. A. & Tanner, J. M. (1969), Variations in pattern of pubertal changes in girls, *Archives of Disease in Childhood, 44*, 291–303.

3.   Frisch, R. E., Revelle, R., & Cook, S. (1973), Components of the critical weight at menarche and at initiation of the adolescent spurt: Estimated total water, lean body mass and fat, *Human Biology, 45*, 469–483.

as we have already mentioned, is thought to be triggered by this change in body fat composition.

The Puberty Holding Pattern

Dr. Michelle Warren first documented delayed pubertal progression in young ballet dancers, finding that while pubic hair development (pubarche) was on time, breast development (thelarche) was markedly delayed (all of the dancers in her study showed little or no breast development at thirteen, and three-quarters of her group were still a stage behind in breast development at menarche). Interestingly, not only did progression of sexual development correlate with a decrease in exercise or with injury, but the subsequent rate of breast development was relatively rapid.[4]

Thus, Sara and the other late bloomers we met in the last chapter are not necessarily lean-hipped and flat-chested because these are family traits. Though chronologically they may be eighteen, nineteen, or even in their twenties, they preserve the body configuration of an adolescent who has not made the complete transition through puberty. They simply don't have enough estrogen to kick things off, so like Peter Pan, they can get older without really growing up. And, as we have also seen, even after the onset of menstruation and progression through puberty—like Susan, Eva, or Kathy—they may revert to abnormal or more immature hormone levels and patterns.

Young dancers appear to be no more likely to rate their breast development as "off-time" (late) than nondancers, even though such development is twice as likely to be late in dancers. This is consistent with perceived maturational timing as relative to one's social context; in the dance, late development is viewed as normative. Significantly, breast development is perceived more negatively by dancers than nondancers; in essence, dancers respond to the changes of puberty differently than nondancers.[5]

To the dancer, the most relevant aspect of maturational timing and hormonal patterns is likely to be their relationship to weight control. A

4.   Warren, M. P. (1980), The effects of exercise on pubertal progression and reproductive function in girls, *Journal of Clinical Endocrinology and Metabolism, 51,* 1150–1157.

5.   Gargiulo, J., Attie, I., Brooks-Gunn, J., & Warren, M. P. (1987), Girls' dating behavior as a function of social context and maturation, *Developmental Psychology, 23,* 730–737.

nineteen-year-old dancer whose puberty is delayed will wage a different war with food than her more curvaceous counterpart, who has undergone menarche and developed more "female contours." And the mature dancer, who is no longer in a hormonal holding pattern, may find weight control a much more difficult task than when she was training in professional school. As hormones change, realistic body expectations may be transformed into unrealistic ones.

Consider the case of Ellen, an eighteen-year-old ballet scholarship student who has fairly regular menstrual function. According to a teacher, Ellen has "trouble with her weight." Currently weighing in at 115 pounds, she thinks she looks and feels good at 107, but the consensus is that she must get down to 100 pounds, especially if she wants to be accepted into the company (she is almost five feet, four inches).

Ellen has been in New York for less than three years, and underwent most of her sexual development while dancing regionally. Her goal is to look like her good friend in the school, "who looks like a fifteen-year-old" despite the fact that she is older than Ellen. The friend began ballet training at an early age at an East Coast performing arts academy, and although she is an inch taller than Ellen, she has no problem attaining a weight of a 100 pounds (she would like to stay around 92, however).

"I would give anything to look like her," Ellen told me, and I believe her. Ellen has virtually tortured herself with laxatives, vomiting, and semi-starvation. At the time of our interview, she was pursuing a ridiculous dietary regimen, predominantly of liquids and diuretics.

In the meantime, Ellen's friend expects her first period one of these days, though she isn't exactly holding her breath.

The Metamorphosis Considered

For their part, most eighteen-year-old ballet dancers are not very concerned with their reproductive capabilities, and as far as breasts and periods go, many young dancers don't feel abnormal or exactly heartbroken about the absence of either. Mature dancers are more likely to prefer more breast tissue as they age, as the dichotomy between a dancer's and the woman's body becomes more pronounced and professional priorities begin to shift. But as I have shown, a number of young dancers view maturation and physical development as a definite career threat (this paranoia may be justified), and some face the approach of menarche and breast growth with considerable dread and apprehension. Adolescence implies much more than hormonal change, and physiological development must always be considered in light of the individual's socialization and hence, perceptions and attitudes toward the self. The dance world may shape the mental development of the dancer just as much as it does the physical.

Consider Jane, a twenty-six-year-old dancer in New York City, who began studying ballet seriously as a child but prefers working in jazz. At five feet, four inches, and weighing 109 pounds, Jane doesn't see her body as that of the ideal ballerina. Following are excerpts from an interview:

> *Vincent:* How do you feel about your body now?
> *Jane:* I'm glad that I'm a jazz dancer and not a ballet dancer.
> *Vincent:* Why?
> *Jane:* Because as thin as I get, I have sort of—I don't know—a sexy body. And ballet dancers don't.
> *Vincent:* So you want a sexy body.
> *Jane:* I can't help it, what can I do? [Laughter] How much weight can I lose? [More laughter] You know what I'm saying.
> *Vincent:* (politely) You're . . . uh. . .
> *Jane:* Yeah, no matter how thin I get—I mean my arms will become pins, and I'll still—my bones will stick out to nothing, and I'll still have, uh. . .
> *Vincent:* Go ahead. Say it.
> *Jane:* I'll still have, you know. . .

In this roundabout way, we finally established the obvious fact that Jane has a substantial bustline and a curvaceous body contour despite her thinness. We next discussed her initiation into the ballet world.

> *Jane:* I had always been an extremely thin child. I was incredibly thin. My mother was afraid for me, and I was at—[company school] and everything was great there, and then I started getting pressures and I left.
> *Vincent:* What kind of pressures?
> *Jane:* Well, I was on scholarship. I was only nine years old. And I hated it.
> *Vincent:* Were you thin then?
> *Jane:* Terribly.
> *Vincent:* Because of the pressures?
> *Jane:* No, I was just a very thin girl.

Vincent: Then you wouldn't feel pressure about losing weight if you were naturally thin.

Jane: No, but I always remember being told, "Stay this way. Never gain weight, because you'll never have any troubles."

Vincent: Except you were growing. [The growth spurt is at this age.]

Jane: But I was growing, and they were telling me not to eat, not to do this, so I left, and stopped dancing for about four years, and then I gained a lot of weight. [Then] I got my period—I was very young, about twelve or thirteen.

Vincent: How did you react to your first period?

Jane: I was relieved. Because I remembered thinking, "Now I'm going to get breasts."

Vincent: So you wanted breasts?

Jane: Oh, yes.

Vincent: That isn't the usual . . .

Jane: . . . because I wasn't dancing, remember? I stopped dancing [between the ages of nine and fourteen].

Vincent: So you think if you had continued dancing you wouldn't have wanted breasts?

Jane: Well, maybe. Because I would have been around girls who weren't developing. I was around girls who *were* developing [in public school]. But the most incredible thing is that I developed very quickly. I went from a skinny little girl to *this*.

From looking at pictures of herself as a child, Jane thinks she might have had a very good ballet body, because she was "thin and long." And, she believes, had she not taken the hiatus from classical dance, she might have adopted "a ballet life-style." Had she remained in the company school, maintaining her "natural thinness," would her bustline be the same as it is today? Conceivably her puberty (and onset of menstruation) could have been delayed, in which case she wouldn't have developed that bustline as soon as she did. But can a woman genetically destined to have large breasts actually have a different body configuration because of involvement in dance? The question boils down to whether or not the alterations in developmental progress are temporary or permanent.

This isn't the kind of question that is easy to study, so we can only make educated guesses based on empirical observations. The general consensus among endocrinologists and gynecologists is that it is "never too late" to develop breast tissue, provided there are the appropriate hormonal influences. In a recent clinical report in the pediatric literature, two female patients with primary amenorrhea caused by long-term undernutrition (both patients were severely debilitated and bedridden, with disordered swallowing mechanisms) matured sexually at twenty-four and thirty-three after tube feedings resulted in increased weight and fat.[6] One gynecologist cited a patient who had an undiagnosed congenital abnormality and, consequently, extremely low estrogen levels. After the diagnosis was made and estrogen replacement administered, the woman began her breast development, at the age of fifty-six. [7]

Another gynecologist and researcher related her experience in following several dancers with delayed puberty, some of whom didn't begin menstruating until their late teens and twenties. After gaining adequate weight, they seemed to go through a "second puberty." As she told me, "They suddenly start to develop. Their breasts start to develop, they put on weight, and they look absolutely normal. They go through a metamorphosis—it's amazing."

The Gynecologic Downside

I think ballet dancers have a prolongation of their prepubertal state, and that puberty is just delayed; or they revert to a prepubertal state if they've already started menstruating. And I think that most likely it will turn out to be a reversible thing that will have no long-term effects. That's my impression. I don't know.

Endocrinologist, 1978

When I spoke to this endocrinologist again recently, she was advocating, like many other specialists in the field, hormonal replacement therapy for many of her amenorrheic dancer patients. Menstrual dysfunction in athletes now produces considerable uneasiness in the medical community, since mounting evidence suggests that these hormonal alterations

---

6.   Feigelman, T., Frisch, R. E., MacBurney, M., et al. (1987), Sexual maturation in third and fourth decades, after nutritional rehabilitation by enteral feeding, *Journal of Pediatrics, 111,* 620–623.

7.   The congenital disorder was gonadal dysgenesis or Turner's Syndrome, the key defect being a genetic abnormality of an X chromosome.

may have serious negative health consequences. Let's examine the principal gynecologic concerns and therapeutic approaches first.[8]

We have already observed that menstrual dysfunction in athletes may consist of normal estrogen but diminished progesterone levels (luteal phase deficiency and euestrogenic anovulation) or low levels of estrogen (hypoestrogenic amenorrhea). In the first case, estrogen secretion without the normal protecting counterbalance of progesterone may result in chronic estrogen overstimulation of the uterus, which could eventually increase the risk of development of "endometrial hyperplasia" (abnormally increased growth of the uterine lining) or possibly endometrial cancer. It has also been suggested that chronic anovulatory women might be at increased risk for breast cancer, theoretically also from persistent, unopposed stimulation of breast tissue by estrogen. To protect the endometrium from this excess stimulation of estrogen, replacement therapy with progesterone has been advocated under the appropriate clinical circumstances (alternatively, oral contraceptives will protect the endometrium).

The issue is quite different when women have persistently low estrogen levels, since obviously they will not have a problem with overstimulation of the uterus or breast. But as we have learned, estrogen has a wide range of influences in the body, and the one most germane to this discussion will take us out of the reproductive system and directly to the skeleton (see the next section). When hypoestrogenic amenorrhea is treated, replacement doses of both estrogen and progesterone are administered (oral contraceptives may also be used to serve this purpose).

As far as fertility goes, hormonal induction of ovulation may be required for pregnancy to be achieved in anovulatory athletes. It is believed, however, that short-term exercise-related menstrual dysfunction, if corrected, will not have permanent adverse effects on future fertility. Fortunately, it seems—as far as the dancer is concerned—that the halt in reproductive capability is just a stall.

I should stress here that menstrual dysfunction should always be evaluated by a physician, who must exclude other causes besides those related to exercise. Before considering medical treatment, most gynecologists and endocrinologists will first recommend a decrease in training or weight gain as a means of restoring normal cycles. If this is unacceptable

---

8.   See the following by Shangold, M. M. (1982), Menstrual irregularity in athletes: Basic principles, evaluation, and treatment, *Canadian Journal of Applied Sport Sciences, 7,* 68–73; (1985), Causes, evaluation, and management of athletic oligo-/amenorrhea, *Medical Clinics of North America, 69,* 83–95; (1986), How I manage exercise-related menstrual disturbances, *Physician and Sportsmedicine, 14,* 113–120.

to the patient or is unsuccessful, hormonal replacement may be recommended (depending upon the clinical situation, such as the age of the patient, duration of amenorrhea, and so on).

Bones and Estrogen: A Delicate Balance

Estrogen plays an important indirect role in bone metabolism, serving not only to stimulate closing of the bone growth centers (and thus affecting the growth of long bones) but also to protect against bone loss. Progressive loss of bone occurs naturally with aging, and its rate accelerates in women when hormonal protection is lost at the menopause. A significant loss of bone mass, "osteoporosis," may predispose otherwise healthy women to fractures of the spine or hip, and lead to severe deformity and debility (Figure 24). Since bone mass is established by about age thirty, any situation resulting in less total bone to begin with (failure to attain a peak skeletal mass) or an augmentation of bone loss, could make one more susceptible to early osteoporosis and its grim consequences.[9] What does this imply for the dancer who may be hypoestrogenic for a considerable length of time and thus deprived of the "bone-sparing" properties of estrogen?

Unfortunately, many studies (most involving runners) have documented diminished bone mineral content ("osteopenia") in amenorrheic athletes, the effect upon bone appearing relatively greater in those women with excessively low body weight or fatness.[10] These findings are all the

9. Two excellent, concise reviews: Ayers, J. W. T. (1985), Hypothalamic osteopenia—Body weight and skeletal mass in the premenopausal woman, *Clinical Obstetrics and Gynecology, 28,* 670–680; Goulding, A. (1986), Athletic amenorrhoea: A risk factor for osteoporosis in later life?, *New Zealand Medical Journal, 99,* 765–767.

10. Cann, C. E., Martin, M. C., Genant, H. K., & Jaffe, R. B. (1984), Decreased spinal mineral content in amenorrheic women, *Journal of the American Medical Association, 251,* 626–629; Drinkwater, B. L., Nilson, K., Chesnut, C. H., et al. (1984), Bone mineral content of amenorrheic and eumenorrheic athletes, *New England Journal of Medicine, 311,* 277–281; Lindberg, J. S., Fears, W. B., Hunt, M. M., et al. (1984), Exercise-induced amenorrhea and bone density, *Annals of Internal Medicine, 101,* 647–648; Linnell, S. L., Stager, J. M., Blue, P. W., et al. (1984), Bone mineral content and menstrual regularity in female runners, *Medicine and Science in Sports and Exercise, 16,* 343–348; Marcus, R., Cann, C., Madvig, P., et al. (1985), Menstrual function and bone mass in elite women distance runners: Endocrine and metabolic features, *Annals of Internal Medicine, 102,* 158–163; Nelson, M. E., Fisher, E. C., Catsos, P. D., et al. (1986), Diet and bone status in amenorrheic runners, *American Journal of Clinical Nutrition, 43,* 910–916. Decreased bone mineral content in young ballet dancers has been reported from Hungary in Horváth, I. & Holló, I. (1986), Letter to the Editor, *New England Journal of Medicine, 315,* 1417–1418.

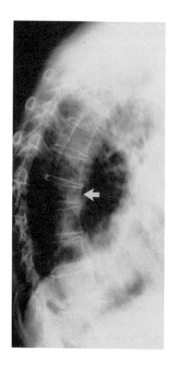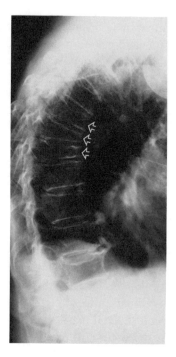

Figure 24. A lateral (side view) chest X-ray of a post-menopausal woman with osteoporosis (left) demonstrates a loss of height and a wedged appearance of a mid-thoracic vertebral body (arrow), representing a spinal compression fracture that is the result of decreased bone mass. In another patient with more severe osteoporosis (right), multiple such fractures are evident (arrows).

more striking given the well-established fact that physical activity in general has a beneficial effect on the maintenance of bone mineral;[11] thus the positive effects of exercise are being overridden. Although there are as yet no studies documenting more spine fractures at an earlier age in this group of women, the fact that the bones of a number of healthy young women have significantly decreased mineral content many years prior to the normal onset of osteoporosis is cause for great concern.

The bulk of evidence points to prolonged low circulating estrogen levels as preventing a large peak bone growth and/or leading to a premature loss of bone mineral. Low estrogen levels alter calcium metabolism in a variety of ways, including decreasing the amount of the calcium-sparing hormone calcitonin, increasing the excretion of calcium in the

11.   Jacobson, P. C., Beaver, W., Grubb, S. A., et al. (1984), Bone density in women: College athletes and older athletic women, *Journal of Orthopedic Research, 2,* 328–332.

urine, decreasing the absorption of calcium in the intestines, and slowing down the metabolism of Vitamin D.[12]

Nutritional factors, however, conceivably also play a role, although there is little hard evidence to substantiate such a relationship. In particular, calcium intake and serum calcium levels have been similar in amenorrheic and eumenorrheic athletes in most studies. Nonetheless, amenorrheic athletes may require more calcium than menstruating athletes, given that low estrogen levels do increase the dietary calcium requirement in postmenopausal women.[13] Increased consumption of nonalcoholic carbonated beverages at the expense of milk, an ever-increasing trend, is a potential factor. (One epidemiological study has identified an increased risk of fractures related to soft-drink consumption).[14] Other possible detrimental effects on bone may be the result of excessive Vitamin A and D intake (which may promote bony resorption); the use of salt tablets (possibly stimulating excessive urinary excretion of calcium); low carbohydrate intake (perhaps leading to a slightly lower absorption of calcium); and high protein intake (which may also increase calcium excretion in the urine).[15] Ironically, dancers have a tendency to drink copious amounts of carbonated diet beverages, overdose on vitamins, subsist on low-carbohydrate, high-protein regimens, and consume less than the recommended amount of calcium, all practices which could add insult to injury as far as the mineral content of their bones is concerned.

The frequency of stress fractures (Figure 25) is significantly increased in amenorrheic athletes as compared to those who menstruate normally.[16]

12.   Ayers, Hypothalamic osteopenia, op. cit.

13.   The daily calcium requirement is 800 mg for adults, and 1,200 mg for growing teenagers. In one study, 42 percent of female ballet students consumed less than two-thirds of the RDA for calcium: see Benson, J., Gillien, D. M., Bourdet, K., & Loosli, A. R. (1985), Inadequate nutrition and chronic calorie restriction in adolescent ballerinas, *Physician and Sportsmedicine, 13,* 79–90; seventeen of twenty-five female dancers in the Cleveland Ballet Company consumed less than 85 percent of the RDA for calcium, and fifteen of these were still deficient despite nutritional supplementation: see Calabrese, L. H., Kirkendall, D. T., Floyd, M., et al. (1983), Menstrual abnormalities, nutritional patterns, and body composition in female classical ballet dancers, *Physician and Sportsmedicine, 11,* 86–98.

14.   Wyshak, G., Frisch, R. E., Albright, N. L., et al. (1986), Carbonated beverage consumption and bone fractures, Abstract, International Symposium on *In Vivo* Body Composition Studies, Sept. 28-Oct. 1, Brookhaven National Laboratory, Upton, Long Island, NY.

15.   Goulding, A., Athletic amenorrhoea, op. cit.; Nelson et al., Diet and bone status, op. cit.

16.   Lindberg et al., Exercise-induced amenorrhea, op. cit.; Lloyd, T., Triantafyllou, S. J., Baker, E. R. et al., (1986), Woman athletes with menstrual irregularity have increased musculoskeletal injuries, *Medicine and Science in Sports and Exercise, 18,* 374–379.

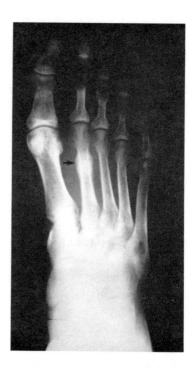

Figure 25. A radiograph of a ballet dancer's foot illustrates the typical appearance of a healing stress fracture of the second metatarsal bone (arrow). The circumferential fluffiness represents callous formation, an indicator of early bone healing. Acute stress fractures, before callous appears, are characteristically not visible with conventional X-rays, and may require nuclear medicine bone scanning for diagnosis. (Case courtesy of Dr. Helene Pavlov, Hospital for Special Surgery, New York City)

Perhaps this association is also the result of decreased bone mineral content in these women, although a causal relationship has not definitely been established, and other factors might be coming into play. In a survey of seventy-five dancers in four professional ballet companies, the total incidence of fractures was 61 percent (of these, 69 percent were stress fractures, mostly in the metatarsal bones); the occurrence of the fractures correlated with increased age at menarche. Additionally, the incidence of secondary amenorrhea was more than twice as high among those with than those without fractures, and the duration of amenorrhea was longer.[17]

17.   Warren, M. P., Brooks-Gunn, J., Hamilton, L., et al. (1986), Scoliosis and fractures in young ballet dancers: Relation to delayed menarche and secondary amenorrhea, *New England Journal of Medicine, 314,* 1348–1353.

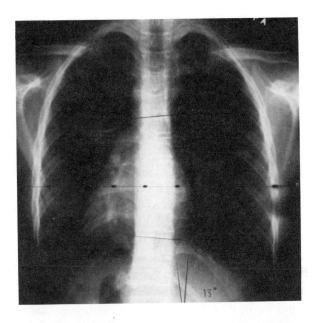

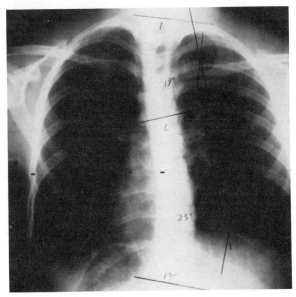

Figure 26. Comparison X-rays of two adolescent girls with scoliosis of the thoracic spine demonstrate a mild curvature (left), and a more severe one (right). Although not demonstrated here, there is a compensatory curvature in the lower spine (in the opposite direction), producing an S-shaped curve.

Surprisingly, the study of professional ballet dancers cited above also found a striking frequency of spinal curvature, or "scoliosis": 24 percent (as compared to a 3.9 percent incidence of scoliosis among Caucasian girls in the general population; See Figure 26). Like stress fractures, the prevalence of scoliosis rose with increased age at menarche, and the dancers with scoliosis were more likely to have secondary amenorrhea (and a longer duration of their amenorrhea) than the dancers without the spinal curvature.[18]

Is this phenomenon also related to diminished bone mineral content of bone due to low estrogen? Although decreased bone accumulation from hypoestrogenism (along with rigorous torso bending exercises resulting in ligamentous laxity) could conceivably predispose one to vertebral instability and curvature, a more plausible explanation involves delayed skeletal maturation. Normally, the progression of spinal curvature in girls ceases at about age sixteen, when the ossification process of spine growth is nearing completion. In dancers, however, the progression of the spinal curve may continue well past sixteen.[19] Thus, delayed skeletal maturation (regardless of mineral content), could allow further expression of scoliosis in this group of females because of the longer growth period. (Let me add that we are not talking about dancing Quasimodos here; the degree of scoliosis in the majority of these dancers is minimal, and not significant enough to warrant therapy.)

The possible implications of low estrogen and bone growth in dancers are fascinating and far from speculative. Since estrogen affects the growth of long bones by stimulating closure of the growth plates, a low-estrogen state in dancers could result in increased height (this is theoretical and has not yet been convincingly shown in dancers) and altered skeletal proportions.[20] In fact, young ballet dancers in the highly competitive New York City setting have been observed to possess a decreased upper-to-lower body ratio and a significantly increased arm span when compared to not only the normal population, but also their

---

18.   Warren et al., Scoliosis and fractures in young ballet dancers, op. cit.

19.   Personal communication from Dr. William G. Hamilton.

20.   Comparison with a variety of uncommon disorders characterized by congenitally low gonadotropin levels (Hypogonadotropic syndromes) is pertinent here, because these patients are usually tall and exhibit so-called "eunuchoidal" features; namely, increased leg length relative to torso and increased arm span (the direct consequences of delayed growth-plate fusion from the absence of sex steroids).

female siblings and mothers (suggesting that these proportions are acquired, not genetic).[21]

Relatively long limbs are coveted features in classical dance, just as assuredly there is no premium for an ample bustline or full hips. Has the sylph become not merely androgynous, but eunuchoid? And given our understanding of estrogen on body contours and proportions, can we convince ourselves that the ideal dancer's body is truly born, and not created?

21. Warren, The effects of exercise on pubertal progression, op. cit. Normally, the length of the upper body and the lower body are equal (lower segment length is obtained by measuring from the symphysis pubis to the floor; upper segment length is then obtained by subtracting this measurement from the total height). Similarly, in normal adults, the arm span is similar to height. In the Warren study, the upper to lower body ratio was 1.01 in the mothers, 1.00 in the nondancing siblings, and .94 in the dancers. The difference between arm span and height in the mothers and siblings was 1.2 centimeters, while it was 2.8 centimeters in the dancers.

8 Two to Tango:
Partnering and Sexuality

*Dancing represents sex in its least costly form, free from imprison-
ment and free to a great extent from the emotional responsibility
and, above all, as a sure thing, independent of someone else's plea-
sure. In other words, it means freedom from sex. The forces which
impelled women to the austerity of the church operate to form the
great dancer. In a strange transmutation dancing is a form of asceti-
cism—almost a form of celibacy.*

Agnes de Mille, *And Promenade Home*

*My experience with these girls is that they couldn't care less about
sex. Even the ones that are married, I think, have very little sex life.*

Physician, New York City

A common misconception equates physicality with sexuality. The
dance is not necessarily sexual, nor do dancers have to be sexual beings.
The absence of sex is perhaps best appreciated in abstract, formalistic

pieces, where male and female are interchangeable as androgynous forms in space. But even when traditional Romantic motifs dominate, a classical dancer need not cast alluring glances at the men in the boxes—a tactic Fanny Cerrito ocassionally resorted to—to evoke sensuality. As André Levinson pointed out, the sexuality is in the movement itself: "What one might also term the classic dancer, is purely functional, serving to facilitate the mechanism of her art. Hence its non-sexual appeal."[1]

Many may find it difficult to separate the work of the artist from the life; the inclination not to do so may be quite overpowering—such is the power of the magic. The manufacturer's representative in the fifth row—entranced by the *pas de deux* from *The Sleeping Beauty*—might squeeze the hand of the spouse of twenty-five years sitting at his side. Afterward, in the glow of the streetlights on Broadway, struck by the intensity of the blueness and time-worn but persistent sparkle of her eyes, he might be prompted to say things not said since days when he was co-captain of the football team and she played saxophone in the marching band at Paseo High School. Aside from an evening of watching fine dancing, these little luxuries alone would be worth the admission price.

But frankly, it isn't really fair to expect as much from the Prince and Aurora once they've taken off their makeup. The Prince's true heartthrob may be waiting at home, or might be that loathsome wicked fairy. And though the two dancers lovingly hold one another, perhaps their sexual preferences don't even jibe; they may feel ambivalent—or even hate each other's guts. Aurora may emerge from the stage door more drained than a boxer finishing a gymnasium workout. She may walk home alone, past the unrecognizing eyes of the manufacturer's rep and his wife, facing the prospects of no other company besides a jacuzzi, a flannel nightgown, and a hungry cat to feed.

In sexual attitudes and behavior, the physiological and the psychological are welded into a human alloy. Because of the subjective nature of sexuality, I initially found myself hesitant to discuss it here, but not only because of the lack of meaningful or pertinent investigations or statistics. What made things worse was the creeping paranoia that at this spot (nearly the shortest chapter in the book), the reader is beginning to pay more attention. I could already visualize a prospective buyer standing in a bookstore, thumbing through immediately to this section. Which undoubtedly accounts for the fact that my writing of this segment has been accompanied by the almost continual sensation that an insect of some sort is crawling under my collar.

1.   Quoted in de Mille, A. (1952), *Dance to the piper*, Boston: Little, Brown, p. 65.

Regardless, the topic is worthy of some mention, as I have been struck by how often the notion of asexuality has surfaced in conversations and interviews. Female dancers, particularly the young serious students of ballet, are not necessarily very sexually oriented. Certainly, I would not be so foolhardy as to generalize about the sexual patterns and attitudes of *all* dancers; the opening quotations must be taken for what they are— subjective impressions from one dancer and one physician. Wishing at all costs to avoid deep-seated, psychological, "internal" explanations to account for these impressions, I want nonetheless to consider some aspects of the dance subculture that might directly or indirectly influence the sexual behavior of dancers. How a particular dancer reacts and is influenced by these factors is an individual concern, defying generalization.

Sublime Sublimation

Socialization aside, the sheer physical work of dance might serve to dampen some sexual preoccupations. Whether the diversion of sexual instincts through dance represents an unconscious choice or whether it is simply an incidental byproduct of the profession is of no matter. Regardless of his motives or psyche, I doubt that Cassanova would have had as much to brag about had he spent his afternoons training for the Boston Marathon. A professional ballet dancer might have eight performances a week for weeks on end, a demand which does not lend itself to carousing until the wee hours of the morning. As a young dancer told me, "Most dancers, when they come home from a day's rehearsal, just don't have the energy to go out and be social butterflies."

Indeed, the major channel through which sexual drive is directed in the aspiring ballerina may be a musculoskeletal one. The need to achieve control over one's body in dance may not just include repression of hunger; it may also include repression of sexual desires and fantasies. Not surprisingly, the serious ballet student may not view herself as a particular "physical" or "huggy" person.[2] Those who aspire to and achieve an asexual body configuration cannot help but desexualize and defeminize themselves as well.

2.   Druss, R. G. & Silverman, J. A. (1979), Body image and perfectionism of ballerinas: Comparison and contrast with anorexia nervosa, *General Hospital Psychiatry, 2,* 115–121.

A well-respected jazz teacher and performer in New York feels that the physical energy expended in dance is very definitely related to sexual energy. Having trained and performed as a classical dancer, she considered the situation of the aspiring ballerina:

> I think they don't realize yet that the energy is sexual energy, and that it can become sublimated if you stay in the ballet, or be conditioned other ways. . . . I didn't have sexual thoughts as young as most people, because my whole world was the ballet, and you see, without realizing it, that kind of physical exercise was releasing the tension anyway, so I wasn't aware of it.

She notices pronounced variations in her own sexual cravings as related to her dancing schedule:

> I know that as long as I dance every day, I'm on a very even keel sexually. But if I stop dancing for two weeks, all I want to do is have sex. I'm so aware, my energy is so intense, God help my husband.

The Sexual Cocoon of the Social Caterpillar

Dancers just don't date as much as nondancers. Many young dancers with an interest in the opposite sex find that the dance cloister has put them in a bit of a quandry. Even if they have the time, the type of social life they desire is simply not readily accessible. The well-insulated dance community may become a cage. Add to this the poor ratio for socialization (the preponderance of females to males), as well as a certain percentage of homosexuality, and things can become tougher.

Explained a company apprentice:

> Gay men can make things kind of difficult. The dance world is a pretty tight world, and you see so many of these people every day that are connected . . . and you don't have that much time to get outside social contacts.

Quipped another about her social life:

> We don't know what to do about it sometimes. What are we supposed to do, stand on a corner? We joke about it a lot.

Time commitments and availability of the opposite sex aside, maturational development (specifically menarchal status) has indeed been shown to affect the dating behavior of dancers. In a study assessing dating behavior of dancers and nondancers, it was found that premenarchal, but not post-menarchal, dancers were delayed in dating compared with nondancers (in the nondance sample, premenarchal girls at each grade level were as likely to date as more mature girls in the same grade). Possible reasons premenstrual dancers date less include: (1) they are subject to less peer group pressure; (2) they have not experienced the change in self-definition that accompanies menarche; and (3) biological factors (hormone levels) are at work.

Conversely, to explain why the postmenarchal dancer might date more, the investigators hypothesized that:

> The postmenarchal dancer may both elicit negative responses from members of the dance world and evoke a different type of environment that better fits her developing physical characteristics. She may lessen her involvement as a function of negative feedback from teachers, negative feelings about physical development, increased external pressure to date, and increased internal desire to date. It may also be the case that postmenarchal dancers become less identified with the ideals of the dance world and begin to date as a compensatory mechanism.[3]

Professional Pressures and Priorities

In a survey comparing fourteen- to eighteen-year-old girls in private schools with those in national ballet company schools, marriage and children were rated as less important by the dance than the nondance students.[4] Avoidance of social involvement may for some be rationalized as a means of guarding against a potential career threat. One young scholarship student told me she stopped seeing her boyfriend because he demanded too much of her time; not himself a part of the dance world,

3. Gargiulo, J., Attie, I., Brooks-Gunn, J., & Warren, M. P. (1987), Girls' dating behavior as a function of social context and maturation, *Developmental Psychology, 23,* 730–737.

4. Brooks-Gunn, J. & Warren, M. P. (1985), The effects of delayed menarche in different contexts: Dance and nondance students, *Journal of Youth and Adolescence, 14,* 285–299.

he didn't, she claimed, "understand" her priorities. A ballet company member in New York City summed up these feelings as follows:

> [Some dancers] feel that getting involved would take away time from their dancing, in which case they wouldn't work as hard, they wouldn't get as many parts, they'd start losing their technique. And in the company it was—not so much now—but it was taboo to get married or even have a boyfriend.

Sounds a bit like shades of the movie *The Red Shoes*. Marriage to both dance and a man may very well be viewed as mutually exclusive, either by the dancer or her artistic director. The conflict between family and career is not by any means unique to contemporary woman in dance, but for the dancer the problems are somewhat special. A professional ballerina who took a hiatus in midcareer to have a baby commented on the company director's reaction: "He would have preferred that I wasn't pregnant. Probably he would have hoped that it would have never come into my mind. Artistically he's right; I mean, what can he do with a pregnant sea nymph?"

Indeed, a pregnant sea nymph is the choreographer's problem, but ultimately the decision to have a child rests with husband and wife and may entail considerable professional sacrifice. Consequently, most professional dancers ardently pursuing their chosen career will place thoughts about a family on the back burner, at least while they're in their twenties.

Balletic Passages

Many of the young girls in New York City who are seriously pursuing a career in ballet were either graduated from high school early (accelerating four years into three), attended a professional performing-arts school, or left their high-school studies incomplete (often to be finished by correspondence or equivalency examinations), thus bypassing typical high-school socialization. Not unusually, they dated either very rarely or not at all in high school: some were just "not interested" and others "too busy," even though they wanted to go out and were often asked.

From talking with large numbers of these students in New York, similar patterns of maturity emerge as almost characteristic of the subculture. When young, the dancers may be more precocious than their peers. Many dance in regional companies, interrelating socially with older dancers either as performers or in dance class. If they are talented and technically advanced for their age, they rank as the youngest members of their classes. They may regard high-school activities as juvenile and a waste of time, a perspective illustrated quite well by Agnes de Mille:

> I was fourteen, and I had found my life's work. I felt superior to other adolescents as I stood beside the adults serene and strong, reassured by my vision.[5]

With advancing age, however, the effects of the cloister become more manifest. In high school the precocious dancer is less involved with her nondancing peers, anxious to leave school behind and get down to the business of dancing. At eighteen, nineteen, and twenty, many seem to lag a bit behind their nondancing counterparts, who, having socialized more extensively in high school, have now gone on to more broadening experiences at colleges and universities or the working world outside of the dance.

The priorities often seem to change in their thirties, when some ballet dancers may find that the restrictiveness of their lifestyle has led them deep into a blind passage. Dancers are neither more nor less vulnerable to career or life crises than anyone else, with one unfortunate exception: at the point when the career of a female professional may just be starting to blossom, the ballet dancer is rapidly becoming deadwood. Once again, I quote Agnes de Mille:

> Whatever the rewards the dancer knows in place of the usual emotional and sexual associations, she is frequently assailed by doubts in her late twenties or early thirties. Even the very great know these morbid spells. The needs of the heart cannot be cheated forever. The dancer grows frightened. The dancer realizes suddenly she is a spinster and aging, no matter how fast she gets around the room. The life of merciless effort, the dimming chances of permanent fame, exhaustion and the growing comprehension of what old age means to a fading athlete without family or home suddenly terrify even the staunchest. The conviction grows that the sacrifice has

5.   Quoted in de Mille, A., *Dance to the Piper*, op. cit., p. 54.

been too much and perhaps not necessary. There is many a volte-face at this point and a marriage with at least one child in a frantic effort to put life back on balance.[6]

Delayed Puberty and Sexual Speculations

The loss of normal sexual desires is a prominent and well-recognized characteristic in the severe emaciation of anorexia nervosa. Does the low amount of "sex fat" in some dancers influence sexuality from a hormonal basis?

I have alluded above to a conceivable association of sexual maturation and dating behavior. Let's look at another possible angle by taking the hypothetical cases of the nineteen-year-old dance student with delayed puberty or a young woman who has reverted to an immature hormonal pattern in association with low body fat. Aside from influencing menar-che and breast growth, remember that estrogen also affects the type of cells lining the vagina as well as the type of secretions. Without appropri-ate stimulation from estrogen, sexual relations could be uncomfortable or less comfortable—a physiological fact that might indeed discourage sexual activity.

In dealing with something as subjective as sexual drive, it is quite difficult to disentangle biological and psychological factors. We have seen, though, that low body weight and the stresses of dancing may affect the levels of sex hormones in the body, and these alterations may be physically manifested in the scheme of things. That such hormonal changes may also modify behavior as well is certainly plausible, though speculative.

---

6.   de Mille, A. (1958), *And promenade home*, Boston: Little, Brown, p. 227.

9 Selection: Darwin at the Mirror

When I have a daughter, I too will keep her clear of competitive ballet schools.

Toni Bentley, *Winter Season: A Dancer's Journal*

Let her get a little pudgy.

New York City dance physician, when asked how he would handle an eleven-year-old daughter serious about ballet.

In the preceding chapters, I have attempted to illustrate how conformance to the expectations of the dance world can literally mold the physical appearance of an adolescent female. The linear, angular body, the small breasts and narrow hips, and perhaps even the relative lengths of limbs and overall height may all be influenced by hormonal characteristics that are themselves determined by rigorous energy demands in combination with the demand for thinness. To what extent, then, is the ballet body "born" or "created?" The question, while not completely answerable, will nonetheless lead us to a consideration of the complex selection process for professional classical ballet dancers.

In general, female late maturers, with longer legs and narrow hips and less relative fatness, are better suited for a variety of athletic disciplines (e.g., running, jumping, throwing), and the success of females with these characteristics might well contribute to the higher average age of menarche which has been reported in female athletes.[1] This isn't so for males—during the years of active growth, male athletes are usually ahead in maturation compared to their nonathletic peers, and generally the good performers are more advanced than poor performers.[2] R. M. Malina has hypothesized that the maturity delay seen in female athletes is primarily attributable to their biological lateness, along with the tendency for early-maturing girls to be "socialized away" from sports participation (while late-maturers are "socialized into" sport).[3]

Cause and effect are not so straightforward for the dancer, particularly for one selected early on by a competitive ballet school. I quote a professional ballet school administrator, with over four decades of experience in auditioning young girls for a potential career in ballet:

> Our teachers . . . have a feel for a little girl's body that is already a little bit too plump for the age. It's very subtle, but it's there. There are some girls that are really developing very fast at a very early age, and we worry that that development is going to continue. And you can see that the girl is going to be a big—you know—well-developed, well-endowed girl.

Translation: Early maturers (menarche at age eleven-and-a-half or younger)—no matter how good their feet, no matter how strong, flexible, or motivated—haven't really got a fighting chance. In fact, of seventy-six females in four national ballet company schools, only 6 percent were

---

1. Malina, R. M., Harper, A. B., Avent, H. H., & Campbell, D. E. (1973), Age at menarche in athletes and non-athletes, *Medicine and Science in Sports, 5,* 11–13; Malina, R. M., Spirduso, W. W., Tate, C., & Baylor, A. M. (1978), Age of menarche and selected menstrual characteristics in athletes at different competitive levels and in different sports, *Medicine and Science in Sports, 10,* 218–222; Malina, R. M., Bouchard, C., Shoup, R. F., et al. (1979), Age at menarche, family size, and birth order in athletes at the Montreal Olympic Games, 1976, *Medicine and Science in Sports,* 11, 354–358.

2. Malina et al., Age at menarche, op. cit.

3. Malina, R. M. (1983), Menarche in athletes: A synthesis and hypothesis, *Annals of Human Biology, 10,* 1–24.

early maturers.[4] Without question, competitive dance-company schools will preferentially select for the body type associated with late maturation. If the first selection occurs early enough (age eight or nine), would-be on-time maturers (between eleven-and-a-half and fourteen years old at menarche) will be indistinguishable from the would-be late ones (menarche at fourteen years and beyond). And regardless of any inherited maturational time-table, young dancers selected are likely to become *later* maturers anyway. As has been shown with other female athletes, age of menarche in ballet students is positively related to the amount of time spent training before menarche, with a delayed onset of 0.44 years for each year of premenarchal training.[5] While 57 percent of ballet students in national ballet company schools are late maturers, the percentage increases to about 70 percent among adult classical ballet dancers in national companies.[6] As one climbs higher up the ladder, late maturation becomes more and more important.

The success of a portion of the selection process does not represent a self-fulfilling prophecy as much as a self-induced one. Late maturers have the competitive advantage, but the system does more than its share to impose that lateness. Accept someone who is either very young or a late maturer, immerse her in the weight-obsessive culture, and you can be fairly sure of delaying her development still further. The need to start classical dance training at a young age involves considerably more than technical development; it hinges equally upon physical nondevelopment.

As we have seen, those dancers whose stage of maturation is "out of sync" will be in an unenviable position when it comes to competing with the sylph. Conformance to the dictates of their special environment is likely to trigger physiologic adaptive responses that make dieting and weight control all the more difficult. Consequently, they run an increased risk of resorting to potentially destructive eating practices. They are also more prone to menstrual dysfunction, and perhaps to alterations in bone composition that could predispose them to musculoskeletal injury. Late maturers who are genetically predisposed to heaviness will fall in the

4.   Brooks-Gunn, J. & Warren, M. P. (1985), The effects of delayed menarche in different contexts: Dance and nondance students, *Journal of Youth and Adolescence, 14,* 285–299.

5.   Hamilton, L. H., Brooks-Gunn, J., Warren, M. P. & Hamilton, W. G. (1988), The role of selectivity in the pathogenesis of eating problems in ballet dancers, *Medicine and Science in Sports and Exercise, 20,* 560–565.

6.   Brooks-Gunn, J. & Warren, M. P., The effects of delayed menarche in different contexts, op. cit.

same category, as will, for that matter, any dancer who attempts to maintain a weight that is unnatural for her as an individual.

A recent study of elite student ballerinas has documented that on-time dance students are less emotionally healthy psychologically than late maturers: specifically, testing reveals more negative body images, higher dieting and bulimia scores, and less oral control (less success with eating restraint).[7] Similarly, in a study comparing "heavier" (-4 to -10 percent below ideal weight) to "thinner" (-11 to -21 percent below ideal weight) professional ballet dancers, the heavier dancers consumed fewer calories (1,343 kcal per day compared with 2,296), exhibited more dieting behavior, and reported more menstrual irregularities than thinner ones.[8]

In an analogous study involving professionals, dancers in three national U.S. ballet companies were compared on the basis of whether they were selected from company schools (with rigid weight and body shape standards from late childhood on) or by general auditions. The less-selected auditioned dancers reported significantly more eating problems (46 percent vs. 11 percent) and anorectic behavior when compared with those rising through the ranks of a company school.[9] An even more telling observation was the incidence of obesity in the dancers' families: 42 percent for the auditioned dancers versus 5 percent for the selected ones.

Thus, despite the fact that the ballet mistress's "feel" really has little to do with an extraordinary ability to identify naturally thin girls, the naturally thin girls will reveal themselves in time because they are more likely to survive the stringent selection process. Recall that only about 5 percent of eight-years-olds at the School of American Ballet will graduate nine years later, and consider that the heat on the selection burners is only beginning to get turned up if one includes traveling through the ranks to soloist or principal status. This is indeed a Darwinian selection, a survival of the fittest (or naturally thinnest), in which genes will ultimately get a shot at expressing themselves.[10] Adaptive responses cannot bridge the gap indefinitely.

7.   Brooks-Gunn, J. & Warren, M. P., The effects of delayed menarche in different contexts, op. cit.

8.   Hamilton, L. H., Brooks-Gunn, J. & Warren, M. P. (1986), Nutritional intake of female dancers: A reflection of eating problems, *International Journal of Eating Disorders*, 5, 925–934.

9.   Hamilton, et al., The role of selectivity, op. cit.

10.   The concept of a Darwinesque selection in ballet originated with Dr. William Hamilton. See: Hamilton, W. G. (1986), Physical prerequisites for ballet dancers, *Journal of Musculoskeletal Medicine*, 3, 61–66.

I have argued that the ideal look may be unnatural for even the naturally thin. But let's be practical and resign ourselves to the way things are and focus on our own best interests. How do we deal with the realities of the dance world and preserve good health? If you've stuck with me this far, I'll assume you might be interested in my opinion, for what it's worth. So what follows is some (almost) free advice (particularly when amortized over the cost of this book) for dancers and their parents.

Face facts

Don't be blind to the realities of the classical dance world, and don't expect those realities to change any time in the near future. A short and squat dancer should not aspire to dancing with the New York City Ballet any more than a five-footer should anticipate playing center for the Los Angeles Lakers.

Appreciate dance for its own value. Dance is not just about performing. The bottom line is that most little girls in ballet class will never be serious dancers. They should be in class to gain the experience of dance and feel good about themselves. Dance teaches discipline, focus, musicality, provides a sense of belonging and group identification, and allows a child a means of expression regardless of verbal abilities, talent, or looks. Dancing should be fun. If a child leaves a dance studio feeling bad about herself, either the teacher has failed or it's the wrong school.

If you're intent upon performing (regardless of level), recognize and accept your physicality, and work within your abilities. Find a type of dance or company that your body is best suited for rather than attempting to overhaul your body.

Be a critical consumer

Anyone who takes dance class or sends a child to dance class is paying for a service. A good teacher will spend as much energy on those who will never dance professionally as those who might, recognizing each student for what she can accomplish as an individual. When a teacher devotes a disproportionate amount of attention to one or two prize students, the parents of the ignored kids are essentially subsidizing someone else's child.

Don't be psyched out by the performing credentials of teachers: success as a performer has nothing to do with the ability to teach. Teaching involves much more than showing steps and correcting position and placement. A good teacher understands how to support and nourish a child, and recognizes that children are not simply small adults. Remember that most dance teachers have no teaching certificates or formal qualifications as teachers, no mechanism for evaluation, and no continuing education. Some may be teaching because they themselves have little formal education and thus have limited career opportunities.

How does a parent without a dance background know if a teacher's any good? Even though one might not understand good and bad technique, at least a parent should be able to recognize a healthy environment for the child. Interview the teacher and sit in on a class before signing up. Look for the negatives: Does the teacher play favorites? Do the same one or two students always get positioned in the front, or lead across the floor? Is a child criticized because of her weight or body type? Is instruction offered with dubious regard for a child's feelings? Is a child subjected to peer group criticism? ["Now everyone, what is Susie doing *wrong* here?" Fifteen eager hands go up.] In essence, does or doesn't the teacher possess the qualities that you would expect in a "regular" school teacher?

Look out for number one

Never assume that a dance school, particularly one associated with a regional or national company, will be making your child's welfare or safety its highest priority. The premises that one takes for granted in other school situations do not necessarily hold in the dance world. Don't expect fairness. Don't waste time trying to make sense of irrational behavior; use your energies to minimize and deal with the hurt. Help your child avoid internalizing blame if she is the victim of arbitrary behavior or decisions.

Your child has no contract or union for protection—you're her only advocate. Don't put your or your child's health on the line for someone else's artistic sensibility unless you're willing to pay the price. (While we're on the subject: anyone who is seriously involved in dance should have more than adequate health insurance.)

Keep the pressures to a minimum

Parents must be aware of the kinds of pressures a child in dance might be subjected to. As a parent, don't make things worse. For starters, don't put your child in the wrong dance environment: a plump, inflexible little girl should not be enrolled in a school associated with a regional company. Regardless of the child's level of dancing, provide support without pushing; distinguish what you wish you could have done from what your child wants or is able to achieve.

Promote cooperation instead of competition by fostering friendships and activities outside of dance class. Understand the selection process and avoid unrealistic expectations. Don't set yourself or your child up for failure, and don't be disappointed (or inflict guilt) if your child chooses to withdraw from the competitive fast lane. Support what is often a very hard decision, and perhaps be relieved that your child is actively choosing and coping with the transition, rather than perceiving herself as a casualty.

Don't put all your eggs in one basket

Explore your options and develop outside interests, alternative strategies, and foci. Hedge your bets by not sacrificing your education. Most dancers are finished performing professionally in their thirties and will spend most of their lives *not* performing. Thus, even those select few who make it professionally must plan for a life beyond dance. Do your planning early.

Beyond the Mirror

In the weight-obsessed dance subculture, those who pass judgment on weight may well be overzealous and their expectations unrealistic. Unfortunately, for too long we as a society have bought the package. Are things changing?

Slowly, perhaps. There are encouraging signs. Some competitive ballet schools are becoming a bit more lenient about weight in the lower levels. Scales are now more often being used to identify the too-thin, not the too-heavy dancer. Performing-arts medicine has come into its own and the negative implications of excessive thinness have become overwhelmingly obvious. The old dictatorial ballet guard is gradually being replaced.

Other cultural trends are coming into play. We are becoming older as a population, and the obsessive identification with youth may be waning. Feminist ideals have undoubtedly had a positive effect, not to mention the growing involvement of women in choreography. Role models are changing as well. We are seeing female track and field athletes returning to competition after having children. We recognize that adolescent gymnasts, despite their technical virtuosity, are not always able to pull off the artistic aspects of a program that require a greater element of maturity. We are uplifted by the continued success of veteran athletes in sports.

Lois Banner has observed that it is a truism of fashion history that any prevalent style normally develops into an extreme expression of form before another style replaces it.[11] That extreme may have reached its culmination in the late 1970s. When interviewing young dancers for the first edition of this book during that period, I made it my practice to end each session with, "Who has the dancer's body that you aspire to or admire the most?" The hands down favorite at the time was Gelsey Kirkland, with Natalia Makarova a distant second. My own personal preferences at the time, Cynthia Gregory and Martine van Hamel (Figures 27 and 28), didn't get mentioned at all. Makarova and Kirkland surely occupied the lean end of the body spectrum (Figures 29 and 30). Ironically, a decade later, Gelsey Kirkland was to publicly reveal her past problems with eating (and drug addiction).[12] Certainly Gelsey Kirkland's story must be viewed as an individual history, not generalized to represent that of the community of dancers. What is more pertinent and disturbing than any individual tragedy, however, is the sad fact that Gelsey Kirkland was the role model for a generation of young ballet dancers.

During the writing of this book I witnessed my own subtle transformation as part of the dance audience. I became uncomfortable and distracted by an angular line of a too-thin dancer. And a common question— "Wouldn't it be better to be five pounds too light than five pounds too heavy?"—which I once answered overwhelmingly in the affirmative, elicited a different response. To begin with, five pounds either way doesn't seem like a national emergency. Second, since emaciation and morbid obesity are equally undesirable extremes, lesser gradations don't particularly tip the scale one way or the other.

To modify our aesthetic sensibilities may take a conscious, individual effort; we should not depend on the arts or fashion to help us adjust our vision. The change need not be drastic or accomplished overnight; it might be as subtle as the visual adjustments that have gradually brought us to our present perspective. Consider a more deliberate look at the Venus de Milo, disregarding for a moment the fashion shows, the magazine spreads, the display window mannequins. Actually, you may think, decked out in the right outfit she might not look so bad after all.

11. Banner, L. (1983), *American beauty*, New York: Knopf, p. 55.
12. Kirkland, G. & Lawrence, G. (1986), *Dancing on my grave,* New York: Doubleday.

Figure 27. Cynthia Gregory in the American Ballet Theatre's production of *Swan Lake*, 1978. (Photo courtesy of William J. Reilly)

Figure 28. Martine van Hamel in the American Ballet Theatre's production of *Don Quixote*, 1978. (Photo courtesy of Deborah Falik)

Figure 29. Natalia Makarova in the American Ballet Theatre's production of *Don Quixote*, 1978. (Photo courtesy of William J. Reilly)

Figure 30. Gelsey Kirkland in the American Ballet Theatre's production of *The Nut-cracker*, 1977. (Photo courtesy of Deborah Falik)

Glossary

Adrenarche: the stage of puberty characterized by an increase in release of hormones from the adrenal gland.

Adrenocorticotropin (ACTH): a pituitary hormone that stimulates the adrenal gland (more specifically, the outer layer or cortex).

Aerobic: refers to processes requiring oxygen.

Aldosterone: the principal electrolyte-regulating hormone of the adrenal gland, primarily concerned with sodium balance.

Amenorrhea: absence or abnormal stoppage of menstrual flow; may be *primary* (failure of menstruation to occur at puberty) or *secondary* (cessation of menstruation once it has been established).

Amino acids: the basic components of protein.

Anaerobic: referring to processes occurring without oxygen.

Anorexia (true): lack or loss of appetite.

Anorexia nervosa: a syndrome characterized by severe emaciation resulting from self-imposed weight loss.

Anovulation: the absence of ovulation.

Anti-diuretic hormone (ADH): a hormone secreted by the pituitary gland that diminishes the amount of urine produced.

Beta cells: the insulin-producing cells of the pancreas.

Blood sugar: glucose circulating in the bloodstream (the form in which carbohydrate is transported in the blood).

Bradycardia: abnormally slow heart rate.

Bulimia: compulsive eating of an extreme nature, usually followed by self-induced vomiting.

Calcitonin: a "bone-sparing" hormone produced in the thyroid gland in response to high levels of calcium in the blood; it lowers the blood levels of both calcium and phosphorus and inhibits bone resorption.

Carbohydrate: a group of organic compounds, including the sugars, starches, and celluloses.

Cathartic: a medicine that quickens and increases bowel evacuation.

Consumption: a wasting away of the body; antiquated terminology for tuberculosis.

Corticoid: a term applied to hormones of the outer layer, or cortex, of the adrenal gland.

Cyclic: referring to normal menstrual cycles.

Dehydration: a condition resulting from the loss of body water.

Diuresis: increased urination.

Diuretic: an agent that promotes urination; commonly called a "water pill."

Dysmenorrhea: pain associated with menstruation.

Electrocardiogram: a graphic tracing of the electric current produced by the contraction of the heart.

Electrolytes: elements which have the property of carrying an electrical charge when dissolved in solution.

Emesis: vomiting.

Emetic: an agent that causes vomiting.

Endometrial hyperplasia: a condition characterized by abnormal excessive thickening of the uterine lining.

Endometrium: the inner lining of the uterus, the structure and thickness of which varies with the phases of the menstrual cycle.

Estrogen: female sex hormone with wide variety of functions, including effects on endometrium, breast growth and development, vaginal lining and secretions, and deposition of body fat.

Euestrogenic: characterized by normal estrogen levels.

Eumenorrhea: normal menstruation.

Fatty acids: body fuel for low-intensity exercise; along with glycerol a component of triglycerides.

Feedback: the return of the end product of a pathway or system to serve as input (either positive or negative).

Follicle (ovarian): the ovum along with the cyst-like structure of surrounding cells which serve to nourish and protect the egg as it matures.

Follicular stimulating hormone (FSH): pituitary hormone acting on the ovary, stimulating the growth of the ovarian follicle.

Gluconeogenesis: the formation of carbohydrate from molecules which are not themselves carbohydrate, such as protein or fat.

Glucose: a simple sugar or monosaccharide.

Glycerol: along with fatty acids, a part of triglycerides.

Glycogen: the chief stored form of carbohydrate, in muscle and liver; used primarily in high-intensity exercise.

Glycogenolysis: the breakdown of glycogen in the body.

Gonadarche: that portion of puberty during which the hypothalamic-pituitary-ovarian axis becomes activated.

Gonadotropins: hormones stimulating sexual glands, i.e., FSH and LH.

Gonadotropin-releasing hormone: a hormone produced by the hypothalamus that control the release of the gonadotropins FSH and LH.

Growth hormone (GH): pituitary hormone with wide range of effects, principal among which includes involvement with normal growth.

Growth spurt: developmental period characterized by rapid increase in height and weight; in the female, it begins at about age eight or nine, peaks shortly before menarche, and is virtually complete one to three years after menarche.

Hormones: chemical substances which have specific effects on a certain organ, or "target.".

Hypoestrogenic: characterized by low estrogen levels.

Hypoglycemia: an abnormal decrease in blood sugar level.

Hypokalemia: abnormally low potassium content in the blood.

Hyponatremia: abnormally low sodium content in the blood.

Hypotension: lowered blood pressure.

Hypothalamus: section of the brain involved with, among other things, water balance, satiety, sleep, and temperature regulation.

Hypothalamic-pituitary-ovarian axis: refers to the sum total of interrelationships involved with maintaining the integrity of female hormonal balance.

Hypothalamic releasing factors: hormones of the hypothalamus that regulate hormonal production of the pituitary gland.

Hypothermia: low body temperature.

Hypothyroidism: deficiency of thyroid activity.

Insulin: hormone secreted by the beta cells of the pancreas, concerned with the regulation of carbohydrate metabolism.

Ion: atom or group of atoms that carry a positive or negative electrical charge.

Lactate: an end product of sugar breakdown in the absence of oxygen.

Laxative: an agent that promotes bowel evacuation; a mild cathartic.

Luteal phase deficiency: abnormally short second portion of the menstrual cycle (after ovulation).

Luteinizing hormone (LH): the pituitary hormone involved in the stimulation of ovulation.

Menarche: the onset of menstrual function.

Menstrual dysfunction: any disturbance, impairment, or abnormality of menstruation.

Menstruation: cyclic physiologic uterine bleeding.

Metabolism: the sum total of all chemical and physical processes, constructive as well as destructive, by which a living organism is maintained.

Misattribution: the attributing of a symptom to an incorrect cause.

Oligomenorrhea: abnormally infrequent or scanty menstruation.

Osteomalacia: relative decrease in mineral content of bone.

Osteoporosis: loss of total bone mass.

Ovulation: the expulsion of a "ripe" ovarian follicle into the fallopian tube for possible fertilization.

Pathologic: indicative of or caused by a diseased condition.

Physiologic: normal, not pathologic.

Physiology: the study of the function of the living organism and its parts.

Pituitary: a small gland at the base of the brain responsible for the secretion of a variety of hormones.

Placebo effect: a diminished perception of symptoms after "treatment" with an inactive substance.

Postmenarchal: refers to a female who has undergone menarche, that is, has begun menstruating.

Premenarchal: refers to a female who has not undergone menarche; that is, has not yet menstruated.

Progesterone: hormone which functions to prepare the uterus for reception and development of a fertilized ovum by stimulating glandular proliferation of the endometrium.

Prolactin: a pituitary hormone which stimulates lactation in mammary glands.

Pubarche: refers to the appearance of pubic and axillary hair.

Purgative: a cathartic.

Pyruvate: an intermediary organic substance in energy metabolism.

Restrained eaters: individuals who consistently resist the urge to eat.

Scoliosis: a curvature in the normally straight vertical line of the spine.

Setpoint: a particular body weight which, in theory, is defended by a built-in body control system.

Steroids: a group name of compounds, included in which are the sex hormones.

Stress fracture: a bone fracture that results from repeated cumulative stresses applied over time.

Syndrome: a set of symptoms occurring together.

Thelarche: the beginning of breast development.

Thermogenesis (diet-induced): the expenditure of energy and production of heat induced by food intake, including the energy cost of digestion and absorption of nutrients and that associated with their transformation or storage.

Thyroid stimulating hormone (TSH): a pituitary hormone that stimulates the thyroid gland.

Index